LOST

LAKE PONTCHARTRAIN
RESORTS & ATTRACTIONS

LOST

LAKE PONTCHARTRAIN
RESORTS & ATTRACTIONS

CATHERINE CAMPANELLA

THE
History
PRESS

Published by The History Press
Charleston, SC
www.historypress.com

Front cover: Lifeboat practice at West End, 1890. *Detroit Publishing Company*.
Back cover, top: West End amusements, 1901. *Detroit Publishing Company; bottom*: Pontchartrain
Beach, 1940. Times-Picayune.

First published 2019

Manufactured in the United States

ISBN 9781467141567

Library of Congress Control Number: 2019935359

This book is dedicated to my parents, Vincent and Meredith Knower Campanella, who provided me with the treasured and unforgettable experiences of spending a part of every summer of my childhood and youth at a camp on Lake Pontchartrain.

CONTENTS

INTRODUCTION

In 1823, residents of Gravesend, New York, organized the Gravesend and Coney Island Road and Bridge Company to create a shell road and bridge with the hope of enticing visitors from the city to their quiet seaside town. By 1830, the company had built a hotel and named it Coney Island House. A few years later, a second hotel was built. The rest, as they say, is history—the beginnings of the most famous resort and amusement site in the United States.

At this time, far south, wealthy residents were traveling from the city of New Orleans to the remote Lake Pontchartrain shoreline. Their road was ready-made—an ancient portage used by Native Americans long before Europeans arrived. The visitors dined, drank, danced, gambled and stayed at a luxurious home that had been converted into a hotel. The Pontchartrain Hotel had lovely views of the lake and its shoreline. Soon after, another hotel was built there, then a shell road. And Spanish Fort on Bayou St. John grew to become "The Coney Island of the South." (West End would later make the same claim.)

A railroad company was established in 1830 to transport visitors (and goods) to the remote settlement of Milneburg, on the lakeshore due east of Spanish Fort. The company built a hotel and bathhouses, and soon the train was busy bringing fun-lovers to a little town that would become known around the world as a cradle of jazz.

During this decade, a similar scenario was playing out at other areas of the Pontchartrain shore. Railroad companies were established, built hotels

Coney Island of New Orleans postcard. *Author's collection.*

and provided other enticements for the purpose of making a profit from pleasure-seekers. Railways also led to new resorts in St. Charles and Jefferson Parishes. And then there were the steamboats, which, beginning also in the 1830s, transported excursionists to and from the shorelines of all the civil parishes bordering the lake. A steamboat ride might include dancing and dining on pleasure trips, but some of the same boats were also used to transport enslaved human beings.

"Build it and they will come" possibly best describes the phenomenon of people traveling to places dedicated to enjoyment and amusement in remote areas. Here we explore a part of how that played out around the shores of Lake Pontchartrain, keeping in mind that what was once remote is now a mere car ride away.

On the New Orleans shoreline, the road that made the attractions accessible via automobiles also led, in part, to the destruction of the two aforementioned resorts. As part of a massive land reclamation project in the 1920s and '30s, these were demolished, their former locations left far from the shore. And when good roads and bridges were built, the steamboats fell out of favor, as did the railways, which first built many of the resorts. One might say that the automobile made them too easy to access, too mundane and too unable to compete with more distant and alluring vacation destinations even farther away. And so, what were busy crowded meccas of entertainment are now "lost"—most of them now surrounded by suburban homes.

This book begins at Spanish Fort on the south shore of Lake Pontchartrain then moves easterly and onward to complete a "trip" around the perimeter of the lake, ending at West End in New Orleans. It is not a comprehensive history but a glimpse of places now gone. There are likely mistakes here, but every effort was made to present information as accurately as possible.

1

SPANISH FORT

Every facet of this city's history—from the French colonists to the beginning of Jazz—are linked with the old Spanish Fort area, and we need a community-wide effort to protect and preserve it.
—*Mrs. Victor H. Schiro,* Times-Picayune Dixie Roto, *October 31, 1976*

We begin at Bayou St. John, where, in 1699, natives guided the first Europeans after having led them from the Gulf of Mexico, through the Rigolets and into Lake Pontchartrain. The original inhabitants had long used this route for transport and trade and settled along the shores of the bayou. At the land end of this tributary, they used an ancient path (Bayou Road) to what is now the French Quarter of New Orleans at the Mississippi River. The newcomers first settled among the natives along the bayou before migrating toward the river to establish the city.

The French built Fort St. Jean in 1701 at the mouth of the bayou to protect the settlement from attack via the lake. Archaeologists, under contract to the Federal Emergency Management Agency (FEMA), in 2013 surveyed land near the fort and while doing so found pottery shards from the late Marksville period (AD 300–400), animal bones and pieces of clay tobacco pipes. The team also discovered that Frenchmen had scooped the top from a Native American shell midden and used it as the foundation of their fort.

After Louisiana passed into Spanish ownership, in 1779, a brick fort was erected on the site. Shipping vessels dropped anchor offshore in deeper water; smaller boats conveyed goods via the bayou to the Spanish Custom

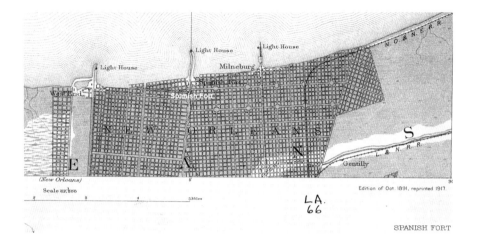

Spanish Fort's location on the south shore is shown in this 1891 U.S. Geological Survey map. *U.S. Geological Survey.*

When the New Orleans Railway and Light Company owned Spanish Fort, it touted the comparison to Coney Island in this 1919 advertisement. Note the bandstand "way out over the lake." Times-Picayune.

House on its shore. A third fort replaced the second in 1808, when the U.S. government built the sturdy structure, now in ruins, along the western edge of the bayou between Robert E. Lee Boulevard and the lake.

In 1803, the U.S. Congress declared New Orleans a port of entry and delivery and the town of Bayou St. John a port of delivery. In 1811, the federal government allocated $2,000 for the construction of a lighthouse there, the first built in the United States outside of the thirteen original colonies. The fort was decommissioned in 1823 but is best remembered as "Spanish Fort," a term used today to describe not only the crumbling remains of the ancient structure now set far back from the lake but also the stretch of land from it to Lake Pontchartrain.

The original access to and from the city to the mouth of Bayou St. John was later complemented by the addition of a shell road, the Carondelet Canal, railroads, streetcars and steamboats. These all allowed the area to become a resort—close enough for a day trip— where food and drink, concerts and dances, picnics and tent shows, mechanical contraptions and alligator rides and much more amused visitors for decades.

The Setting

Sometimes, the prose of the day best sets the scene, flowery as it may be.

> *Where the old Bayou St. John enters the lake, at a point known as the old "Spanish Fort" a beautiful pleasure resort has been created. Extensive and magnificent gardens have been laid out upon made land far into the lake, ornamented by shady walks and pathways, with grottoes and fountains, with cool arbors and sheltered nooks, with the music of excellent bands. The children can find delight in swings and goat carriages, in aviaries and cages of animals, or can amuse themselves by watching the little fish in the aquariums or the big lazy alligators in the ponds. Upon the grounds are fine large hotels and restaurants. A way out over the lake, built upon piles, is a large open air theatre or opera house. The best opera bouffe or burlesque talent, that can be induced to come to New Orleans in the summer gives nightly and matinee performances here, which the audiences enjoy while at the same time inhaling invigorating salt breezes from the Gulf. And the cost of*

all this, railroad fare to and from the city, amounts to exactly 15 cents, a surprise to old-timers, who used to think themselves fortunate if they saved anything from the wreck of a $20 note after a shell road trip to the same place. (Boston Herald, *July 12, 1884*)

Pontchartrain Hotel

An act of Congress in 1819 "authorized the sale of certain military sites" that were deemed "no longer of use" and so Spanish Fort became private property. An early reference to this location as a resort comes from Bernhard, Duke of Saxe Weimar Eisenach, in *Travels through North America During the Years 1825 and 1826*: "Behind the fort is a public house called Ponchartrain [*sic*] Hotel, which is much frequented by persons from the city during summer. I recognized the darling amusements of the inhabitants in a pharo [faro, a gambling card game] and roulette table." Eisenach added that the fort had been abandoned and that "a tavern is now building in its place."

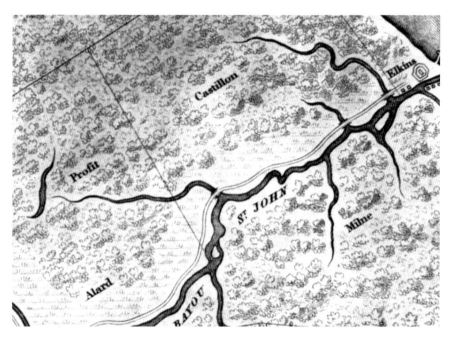

Harvey Elkins took possession of the Spanish Fort property in 1823. However, he did not obtain the title from the government until 1831. *Boston Public Library.*

By 1828, the building was for sale, along with "all furniture, kitchen furniture, seines, canoes, ferry…for stock in trade.…For the rent of the house apply to Mr. Bernard Genois." It is difficult to find historical references to this hotel, but by Eisenach's writing it seems that it was located in a different site than the Bayou St. John Hotel (see below).

In 1867, E. Roger and Company advertised for rent the "Old Fort Hotel," suitable for a residence, hotel or restaurant, located in "the most delightful gardens in the region, full of choice plants and shrubbery, surrounding an ancient mansion" with access via the Carondelet Canal and bayou or along the shell road—"unsurpassed for a pleasure ride."

The Canal Street, City Park and Lake Railroad, according to a September 1, 1874 *Daily-Picayune* report, was in the process of repairing the *"ancient hotel at the fort"* (the Pontchartrain) of which "in front stretch away the waters of the lake…and *on the eastward*, in close proximity to the parapet of the fortification" Given this description, the Pontchartrain Hotel would have been located near the fort, and due to the use of the word *ancient* (the Bayou St. John Hotel was only about forty years old in 1874), it is suspected that the old hotel was built many years before the Bayou St. John Hotel.

Bayou St. John Hotel

In 1823, Harvey Elkins built the posh Bayou St. John Hotel within the walls of the fort (as per Eisenach's description). In doing so, his workers destroyed the fort's brick battery and blockhouse (built in 1809), parapets, gun encampments and part of the inner wall. The hotel was a framed two-story building with a porch on all sides.

Elkins sold the properties, which included the hotel and other buildings, to a group of friends (John Slidell among them) who allowed him to continue to operate the facilities. This syndicate formed the very exclusive Elkin Club comprising wealthy New Orleans movers and shakers. They renamed it the Spanish Fort Hotel, hired a chef and rode from town along the shell road to dine in elegance, gamble, drink and host lavish dances. The Elkin Club is believed to be the first of many private social clubs in the city, but it abandoned Bayou St. John in 1837.

During the 1840s, the Bayou St. John Hotel was again offering bathing, billiards, shooting facilities, food and drink. It came to be known for a time

All that remained of the Bayou St. John Hotel in 1933 were its steps, which led into what had been the fort. *Library of Congress.*

as the "Old Fort House," still serving good food and liquor. By 1845, two bathhouses had been built on the shore.

In 1845, the Millaudon family took over some of the Spanish Fort property and used seven acres for a fine orange grove. In 1850, they sold the property. Their grand home was converted into a resort hotel with fine food operated by A. Levrot. In the late 1850s and '60s, it became the Carondelet Hotel, operated by Alfred Demarine. More bathhouses sprang up by 1859.

A good description of the property can be derived from a March 21, 1868 auction offering for sale "a public resort and comfortable summer and winter residence"—"Old Spanish Fort" and its ten arpents (an old French measurement slightly smaller than an acre) with 419 feet on the lake. It included an extensive two-story framed cypress dwelling containing twenty rooms and front and rear galleries 100 feet long "offering one of the prettiest marine views of the lake imaginable" enclosed by an iron fence. There was also an "extensive building in the rear" of the property, a large vegetable garden and orchards containing three hundred trees—orange (which reaped $3,000 the prior year), Japanese plum, grape and other fruit trees. The hay grown there had brought in $100 the previous year. Also included were three cisterns with a forty-thousand-gallon total volume.

In the 1880s, it was known as the Saiter Hotel, run by W.S. Saiter, who also managed the fort property. Saiter's advertisements boasted, "The largest and best appointed…most liberally managed hotel, restaurant, and gardens…the Only first-class resort near by New Orleans.…The largest summer theater in the world." In that theater he ran an acting company and hosted the Alice Oates Opera Company every evening, with Saturday and Wednesday matinees. His restaurant, in 1883, served Sunday breakfasts and daily dinners. In 1885, Saiter's license was revoked for permitting gambling, and Moses Schwartz took over for a mere $125—there were reportedly few other bidders.

By 1897, the hotel had been leased to L. Smith, who intended to use it as a grocery store and barroom. But before he opened his new business a fire burned the building to the ground, destroyed the wharf along the shoreline and damaged the nearby oak grove.

The Fort

Although Harvey Elkins had partially destroyed the fort in the 1820s to build his hotel, Moses Schwartz restored parts of it in the 1880s, but faulty workmanship resulted in crumbing bricks. While surrounded by the amusement resort, the remains of the fort were a curious attraction. But little was done to maintain its remains.

After the resort was shut down in the 1920s, it was abandoned except for picnickers. In 1938, funds from the Works Progress Administration (WPA) were allotted for excavation and restoration to 1810 conditions. Workers found the bones of "Sancho Pablo" (reputedly a Spanish soldier who fell in love with a Native American maiden, was killed by her outraged father and was buried near the tree where he was slain). The bones are now held by the University of New Orleans anthropology department. WPA workers also made minor repairs to the fort until funds were depleted without completing the effort.

In the late 1930s and the 1940s, as homes were built nearby, residents were prone to take bricks from the ruins to use for patios and other home improvement projects. In the latter half of the twentieth century, young people partied and picnicked there. In the mid-1970s, "Sunny" Shiro, wife of former mayor Victor H. Schiro, led the Spanish Fort Improvement Project for Restoration. She hoped to create an outdoor museum, serenity park and improved lighting. She asked residents to return memorabilia they had gathered from the park. In the 1976 Halloween edition of the *Times-Picayune*, she is quoted as saying, "I've heard that the fence from the Saiter Hotel of 1895 is now located in the 2900 block of St. Charles Avenue and that at least two homeowners in the Lake Vista area proudly admit that their barbecue pits are made of bricks from Fort St. John." Schiro's efforts were in vain. At the time of this writing, the fort and surrounding area lay dormant.

1870s

Beginning in this decade, the railroads owned the rails, rights-of-way, land and most of the improvements at Spanish Fort, which suffered through a series of owners, some much more serious and adept at maintaining, improving and operating a resort than others. The first, in 1873, was the New Orleans, Spanish Fort and Lakeshore Railroad, organized by Moses Schwartz, who owned a New Orleans foundry that produced railroad engines and supplies. This railroad ran from Canal at Basin Streets to the lake.

By 1876, the business was bankrupt, and in 1877, it was sold to the Canal Street, City Park and Lake Railroad, whose president was Thomas H. Handy. It employed a coal-fired dummy engine ("dummies" attempted to disguise railroad engines by enclosing them in what looked like streetcar bodies) that pulled a car equipped for fifty-two passengers. Its route went from Basin Street to Iberville to North St. Patrick, veered along the Orleans Canal (now Orleans Avenue), skirted along City Park, then headed out to the lake. The six-mile trips, made every twenty minutes, lasted about thirty minutes, with stops at the park. The railroad also planned to build a freight wharf, to deepen the bayou to accommodate larger vessels and to add a thirty-foot-wide embankment along the lakeshore.

In 1879, Moses Schwartz rebought the railroad for $7,000 at a sheriff's sale and renamed it New Orleans, Spanish Fort and Lake Railroad. He began hosting concerts (he was the bandleader), built a three-hundred-by-sixty-foot music hall; added three picnic pavilions, a winter garden and a skating rink; and improved the bathhouses. In 1880, he constructed a new grotto with a central prismatic fountain. He hosted fireworks shows and dug a new lake to be stocked with swans and containing a center island featuring an iron fountain depicting a four-foot-tall boy holding a ragged boot with water running through it, often titled *The Unfortunate Boot*. Through the years, copies of the fountain could be found at Children's Hospital, City Park near the Peristyle and the McFadden home in the park (now Christian Brothers Academy).

More that one hundred years before New Orleans World's Fair gondolas crossed the Mississippi River, in 1879, New Orleanian James A. Collins received a patent for cigar-shaped "Balloon Cars," by which he planned to transport goods and people between Spanish Fort and West End. Ten persons at a time would float aloft in a "box" that dangled from each balloon, which would be pulled along the lakeshore via a "tramway," thus creating a "delightful promenade in the air." No record of the balloon cars in use has been found by this author.

Noy's Restaurant

Spanish-born brothers Lorens and Ramon (who was nicknamed "Noy") Alberti opened this restaurant shortly after the first railroad began bringing passengers to Spanish Fort, around 1874, on the eastern shore across the bayou from the fort (or "over the Rhine," as locals called the area). It was renowned for its romantic garden setting, fine Spanish and French food and an exceptional redfish baked with fresh tomatoes, pimentos, olives, capers and shrimp. In 1884, a fire destroyed the restaurant and barroom. A subsequent 1908 fire resulted in the loss of the business as well as most everything else over the Rhine. But the restaurant was rebuilt each time. Ramon Alberti died in 1922, but his children continued to conduct the business.

1880s

Electric lights were introduced to Spanish Fort in 1880. Most folks were delighted, but a complaint was issued in the April 28, 1880 edition of the *Times-Picayune* that they were "so bright a fellow cannot flirt with his girl in a corner without becoming a spectacle." The Casino, popular for refreshments and entertainment, opened in the early 1880s. (The Casino was not a gambling house—"casino" was used back in the day to denote a place to find refreshments and perhaps amusements.) Refreshments on the 1883 Casino menu included turtle soup, red snapper au gratin, chicken à la creole, roast ribs of beef, vegetables, ice cream and fruit.

The Brotherhood of Telegraphers held a ball there in 1880, as did the Young Men's Excelsior Benevolent Association to raise funds for its grand tomb in Metairie Cemetery. The "Young Men" enjoyed a festival that also included an opera, a promenade concert and a pyrotechnical exhibition. For the main event, the Casino was decorated with flowers and bunting, and Wolfe's brass band provided the music. Nightly concerts by the Spanish Fort Orchestra with dancing at the Casino took place in 1889. In 1890, the Crescent City Social Club held a promenade in the gardens, with dancing in the evening.

The first "house band" at Spanish Fort was led by its owner and operator, Moses Schwartz, from 1879 to 1880. William Borchert's band took over the role from 1881 to 1885. In 1886, Professor G. Sontag, who led a marine band in France, conducted the military-style, thirty-member Spanish Fort Band. Its uniforms were inspired by French navy suits. Some were members of the Mexican Band and others of the French Opera House Orchestra.

During the 1880s, Spanish Fort provided, without cost, the Criterion Comic Opera Troupe's presentation of *The Mascot* in nightly and matinee performances (1882), violinist Professor Henry Joubert accompanying vocalist Mrs. B.S. Forcheimer with the Spanish Fort military-style orchestra (1883), the Mexican Typical Orchestra and the St. Quinten Opera Company (1885). The Spanish Fort Opera House sat far out into the lake, built on pilings, and it offered a delightful venue for these performances.

In 1880, when West End was becoming a rival, Spanish Fort began to fall out of favor. The railroad and grounds were transferred to the Erlanger Syndicate (which controlled the New Orleans and Northeastern Railroad Company) for $290,000. Moses Schwartz acted as director and J.M. Siexas as president. In 1881, a new Casino was built.

Left: Philip Werlein published this sheet music from his store at 135 Canal Street in 1886. Note the caboose of the Spanish Fort railway passing through the entrance. *Author's collection.*

Below: An invitation to the 1882 Independent Order of the Moon Carnival Club party, to be held "Once again!" at Spanish Fort. *Author's collection.*

Before introducing mechanized amusement park rides, in 1884, Spanish Fort offered goat carriages for children as well as rides on the backs of the tamer residents of the alligator ponds. At this time, there was a theater, a concert/opera hall and improved gardens. The "Colored" State Fair came to Spanish Fort in 1887.

In 1889, Frederick Knowland secured a ten-year lease on the resort and began to make improvements to the properties and the railroad with promises to run it on frequent schedules and to restore the resort to first-class condition. He also converted the opera house into a theater. The following operas, light as some may be, were presented: *Bells of Corneville*, *Erminie*, *Fra Diavolo*, *The Mikado*, *Olivette*, *H.M.S. Pinafore*, *Roccaccio* and *Said Pasha*.

Over the Rhine Restaurant

In 1880, German-born Otto and Annie Touche opened the Over the Rhine restaurant and bar on the east bank of the bayou across from the resort. No bridge existed, so Otto ferried customers across. In 1866, Otto improved and remodeled his business. With time, sons Fred and Otto Jr. took over and then passed it on to third-generation Freddie Touche. Annie continued to work there until it was lost to the land reclamation project, which relegated its original location as part of Lake Terrace subdivision.

A popular attraction at Over the Rhine was a Civil War submarine built around 1861 on the banks of the bayou. In 1878, without knowledge of its whereabouts, it was accidentally dredged up near the mouth of the bayou and left on the bank until, in 1895, it was placed on display on a wooden berth by the restaurant. In 1908, it was moved to Camp Nicholls Confederate Home on the bayou. In 1942, it was acquired by the State Museum and moved to Jackson Square, then into the lower Pontalba Building, where it was featured in a "Defense Exhibit." In 1957, it was moved under the Presbytere arcade and finally came to rest at the Louisiana State Museum in Baton Rouge in December 1999.

1890s

By the 1890s, a complete amusement park awaited visitors, but its popularity was again fading in competition with West End. During the first half of this decade, it was more or less closed as a resort but became a popular venue for "Negro" picnics and events. In 1893, the annual campfire of the Grand Army of the Republic of New Orleans (a black organization that had been asked to speak at Jefferson Davis's funeral) was held. This organization had eleven local posts and a membership of 897. They brought their own refreshments to dine at the Casino and dance to a brass band. An estimated 5,000 people were in attendance. In 1897, African American baptisms drew large crowds. In 1898, the Onward Brass Band performed in a free concert and dance.

During this period, Spanish Fort had a menagerie of caged and penned animals, including these alligators photographed in 1891. *J.F. Jarvis.*

Brass bands became more popular in the 1890s, when the Pelican Brass Band and Red Men's Brass Band performed in 1891. The Fisher String Band entertained in 1892. The Blind Band, led by Professor Adolph Bothem featuring blind singer/musician C. Murry, drew crowds in 1895, as did Torsiello's Band and the First Artillery Band of Kansas City, Missouri, in 1896.

The East Louisiana Railroad took over and made improvements in 1896. Its president, lumberman John Poitevent, had plans to connect Spanish Fort with his St. Tammany holdings. He built a wharf and a half-mile train trestle into the lake for his steamer *Cape Charles* to run to and from Mandeville. The boat burned at its dock the same year. The following year, the resort was again closed.

1900s

Spanish Fort was more or less closed again between 1900 and 1910 due to both neglect and nature. A 1901 storm badly damaged or ruined the Hot Air Club, Sumpf's Club, Labeaud's Shipyard, Alciator's Place, James Conner's stables and bathhouses, Lone Oak Club, Otlong bathhouse, Andrew Garner's Washington Bathhouse, Defender's Club and the Klondyke Clubhouse.

In the early 1900s, a China tree grove surrounded the Casino and served as the amusement garden. After a 1906 fire destroyed the Casino and five attached buildings, a dancing pavilion took its place as the venue for free open-air performances—opera, light and comic opera, symphony orchestras, military-style bands, solo music concerts, vaudeville, burlesque and, finally, jazz.

The property changed hands several times among different railroad companies. In 1906, the New Orleans Terminal Company was in control. In 1909, the New Orleans Railway and Light Company took over the forty-acre tract for $35,000 and planned a belt rail system from West End to Spanish Fort, updated to an electric rail line, made many improvements and added new structures. This company first introduced amusement park rides, including a Ferris wheel and roller coaster. By 1911, Spanish Fort was in good shape.

1910s

A September 11, 1958 *Times-Picayune* "Up and Down the Street" column by "The Want-ad Reporter" tells us that the estate of Charles W. Weinhardt, said to be the operator of the original Spanish Fort amusement park, was up for auction by Morton Goldberg. Included were crank-turned nickelodeons featuring *The Sin of Beer*, which showed hatchet-armed women destroying saloons à la Carrie Nation; Mack Sennett's pie-tossing bathing beauties; cross-eyed Ben Turpin; and the queen of vamps, Theda Bara. There was a talking scale that verbalized one's weight, strength testers and many other interesting gizmos from days gone by.

On March 26, 1911, streetcars began running to the resort, and a new concrete station was built for them. Part of the boardwalk was covered to protect patrons from the elements while viewing the bandstand. Nightly entertainment included a vaudeville show, moving pictures and Professor

Fitchenberg's Penny Arcade, circa 1910. Herman Fitchenberg was a well-known early motion picture advocate who also owned the Plaza, Alamo and Dreamworld theaters. *John Teunisson.*

Val Leonard became the manager of the new Casino, constructed on the old site that, in 1912, housed musicians, moving pictures, vaudeville shows and Joseph Reno's Restaurant. *Library of Congress.*

A 1912 H.J. Harvey postcard of the entrance to the over-the-water bathhouse. *Author's collection.*

Henriques de la Fuente ("the leader of the French Opera Orchestra… from the Metropolitan opera company of New York") leading a symphony orchestra that continued to perform regularly until 1912.

Early on, the flying horses / carousel was an attraction, but it was moved in 1911 to City Park in Baton Rouge. Some of the "animals" later made their way to New Orleans City Park. A new carousel replaced the original. In 1912, the midway was known as the "Pasco." New attractions of 1913 included "The Great Dip," also known as "The Big Dipper," a roller coaster offering "a mile of thrills in less than a minute." Alleged to reach eighty miles per hour, it was built by Briening and Company. Also included were the Cycle / Circle Swing, the Whip ("the ride that made Coney Island famous" ran on an oval path that spun and jerked), the Caterpillar ("a lark in the dark…riding under cover in the dark at a rapid speed in an artificial cyclone") and the Penny Arcade / Wonderland (now with three hundred attractions, including electric shock and a penny bowling alley). A 1915 storm took down the Ferris wheel and the roller coaster.

Countless forms of amusement were offered to visitors to Spanish Fort. The new automobile road built in 1913 allowed people to more conveniently arrive there to see, for instance, contortionist "The Great Holman" (also known as the "Happy Frog"), a pianologue (comedy with piano accompaniment) by Kate Fowler, rope tricks and a professional whistler.

Professor Emile Tosso's Military Band played here in 1911 and for several years after. The opera *La Perichole* was presented by the Spanish Fort Opera Company in 1912. The next year, a bandstand was again built out in the lake and furnished with electric lighting and benches. George A. Paoletti and his orchestra were the "house band" between 1914 and 1917. The second opera house was demolished around 1914, and the Casino was converted into a dance hall.

A 1915 storm destroyed half of the park, but not before the films of Charlie Chaplin and other moving pictures were shown. Music included ragtime and more, while dancers moved to the tango, the one-step, the foxtrot and the cakewalk—they even square danced. Swimming and fishing from the pier, an Old Folks' Carnival and Country Dance and dance contests for the more youthful crowd were all offered at no charge.

There were baby ostriches at the dancing pavilion in 1916, when Myrtle Howard performed the "ostrich walk" and "ostrich glide" (after having spent much time at the New Orleans Ostrich Farm at 615 City Park Avenue observing the birds) in "Uncle Hiram's Barn Dance," an act that allegedly attracted one thousand to two thousand people. Eggs laid on the farm were displayed at Spanish Fort, and the arrival of new chicks was anxiously awaited. But the throngs were disappointed to learn that the first ostrich ever born in New Orleans had hatched not there, but on the farm. Comedians performed while folks enjoyed the skating rink

In 1918 and 1919, Armand Piron's Jazz Orchestra was the Spanish Fort "house band." In 1919, a monkey cage escapee bit a boy, fled onto the dance floor, then scaled a post to the ceiling. After much mayhem, the poor creature was shot and killed by police.

Tranchina's at Spanish Fort

Here is Terry Tranchina's place, the finest resort restaurant in the south…[for] enjoying a sea food dinner or Creole dishes.…It will be a pleasure to dance on this floor.…This is a mammoth place. "How many can you seat here?" I asked. "Four hundred," I was told, and "one hundred couples can be on the floor comfortably at one time."…At no other resort around New Orleans will you find sea foods and wild fowl prepared as deliciously as here.
—New Orleans Item, *March 19, 1922*

Beginning in 1878, the Tranchina family was active in the operation of a hotel and restaurant at West End (see chapter 8), where they remained until 1913. But in 1888, Italian-born Terry and Joseph Tranchina opened a restaurant at Spanish Fort, the Cottage, with Miguel Brisolari as chef (see chapter 2 for more about Brisolari). In 1913, the brothers moved to a new, large, low-slung stucco building at Spanish Fort with red-tiled porches, first called Tranchina's Miramar. It hosted banquets for as many as four hundred diners and dancers.

Armand Piron's Jazz Band performed regularly at Tranchina's from 1918 until it closed in 1926 (with a hiatus in 1923 and 1924 to record albums in New York City). In 1924, Piron's orchestra became the house band, composed primarily of jazz greats Paul Barbarin on drums, Henry Bocage on bass, Peter Bocage on cornet, Louis Cottrell on drums, Steve Lewis on piano, saxophonist Lorenzo Tio Jr., Piron on the violin and clarinetist Louis Warnick. Other musicians rotated in and out of the band as needed.

In July 1924, federal Prohibition agents raided Tranchina's without a search warrant. Four G-men climbed through windows and busted down the screen door, entered the very crowded hall and leaped onto tables to smash glasses and dishes. One agent brandished a revolver and shouted, "Don't

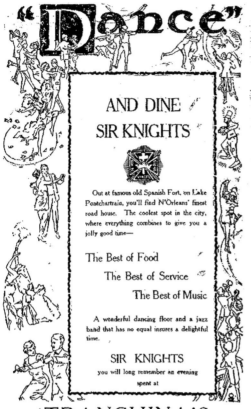

"Dance"

AND DINE
SIR KNIGHTS

Out at famous old Spanish Fort, on Lake Pontchartrain, you'll find N'Orleans' finest road house. The coolest spot in the city, where everything combines to give you a jolly good time—

The Best of Food

The Best of Service

The Best of Music

A wonderful dancing floor and a jazz band that has no equal insures a delightful time.

SIR KNIGHTS
you will long remember an evening spent at

TRANCHINA'S
AT. SPANISH FORT.
Catch Car at Canal and Rampart

Left: An April 25, 1922 advertisement for Tranchina's at Spanish Fort during the national Knights Templar triennial conclave. Times-Picayune.

Below: Armand Piron (*far right*) and his band taking a break during the 1922 Knights convention. *Tulane University.*

move!" to diners and dancers. Women screamed. Men were alarmed. No liquor was found, and the local police arrested the agents, including the divisional chief, for disturbing the peace and disorderly conduct. Of the three hundred patrons, several prominent businessmen acted as witnesses in defense of the police action. They included the presidents of Marks Isaacs and Mayer Istrael department stores, the president of the Cotton Exchange and the future president of the Orleans Levee Board, Abe Shushan.

In 1924, Felix Tranchina was not only the proprietor of the restaurant (where the Tuxedo Jazz Band was playing) but also manager of the resort, along with Crescent Amusement Company (operator of the rides and concessions). At that time, Tranchina also had a bathing pavilion with dressing rooms, towels, lockers, bathing suits, waterslides and chutes.

The renowned restaurant, a cradle of jazz, ended its glory in 1925 when the the venue was remodeled and converted into a Japanese-style dance hall named Tokio Gardens (the second venue so named; see later in this chapter).

An aerial view of Spanish Fort in 1922. *New Orleans Levee Board.*

1920s

In 1920, cyclist Frank "Dare Devil" Doherty awed the crowed with his "Leap for Life." The following year, Oscar "The Great" Babcock did a loop-the-loop around a giant, upright, circular track.

The Spanish Fort house band in 1920 was Tosso's Jazz Band, followed by Happy Schilling's Jazz Band in 1921, then Peter Pelligrini's Jazz Band and Santo's Palace Orchestra in 1922. In 1923, Johnny Bayersdorffer's Jazz Band shared the spotlight with Piron but continued on as the steady performers until 1925. The final house band at Spanish Fort was Joe Loyocano's Jazz Band.

In 1920, new attractions included the "Old Mill Stream" (small boats inside an oval underground tube-like structure propelled by the mill wheel) and boat rides with "Negroes playing banjos and singing." The Frolic and the "Ball-in-Jack" rides were added in 1921. A new

Bathhouse and water chute, 1922. *Unknown source.*

roller coaster was erected in 1922, and the Dodge 'Em (what we now call bumper cars, "with all the excitement of a train-wreck and none of the dangers") opened. In 1922, an old-timer remembered when there were attractions named the Bicycle Race and the Aeroplane Swing, a bathhouse accommodating three thousand people and when men and women would "ride the surf boards down the toboggan and fly out over the water." In the 1920s, there were reportedly large crowds enjoying vaudeville acts, minor musical performances and local singer Willie Jackson, who performed regularly at the Casino.

In July 1922, some flappers and their beaus were amusing one another at "petting parties" while others were partaking in "delirious dancing." Spanish Fort concessionaire the New Orleans Railway & Light Company installed additional lights in the dance hall and imposed "eagle-eyed demon chaperones all over." "They shall not wriggle" was the mandate. Such actions would be "ruthlessly stopped by a newly-appointed censor," said Bloor Schleppey, press agent for the company. Schleppey also

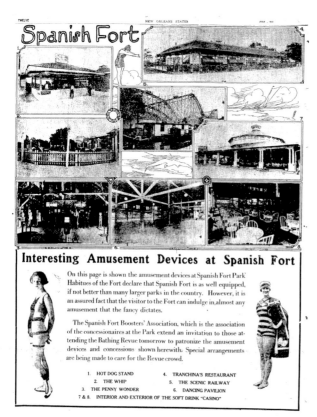

"Interesting Amusement Devices" are touted in this July 2, 1922 advertisement. *New Orleans States.*

Cyclist Loop Babcock circles the "Death Trap" in the "Greatest Act Ever Shown at Spanish Fort" in this June 8, 1923 ad. Times-Picayune.

reported that "complaints have been filed about some of the rough stuff that has been pulled at the Spanish Fort Park. These conditions will not be tolerated."

The Spanish Fort Radio Station was formally dedicated in 1924 with the call letters WEBP. It was owned by New Orleans Public Service Inc. (which was then the owner of the resort) and the Crescent Amusement company. At the ceremony, a talk on "Safety" by NOPSI president Herbert B. Flowers was followed by a musical program broadcast to the estimated fifteen thousand radio receiving sets in the city. Tosso's band, Bayersdoffer's dance orchestra and the Tuxedo Jazz Band from Tranchina's restaurant all performed. Willie Jackson sang several songs.

Kid's Day in 1924 included games and races, free entertainment and candy and half-priced rides. In 1925, there was a Boob McNutt Crazy House (based on a character of Rube Goldberg's cartoon series). To attract more visitors, Crescent Amusement offered prizes and other incentives, including an automobile giveaway. A July 1924 *Times-Picayune* article noted that the promenade pier leading to the pavilion was "unusually crowded with spectators watching the swimmers riding on the giant plunge…which has become one of the most popular attractions at the park." The Penny Arcade was also a well-visited place for family amusement, and Emile Tosso's band attracted sizable crowds. The paper also reported that "on two days, July 4, and July 14, 1924 more than 40,000" attended Spanish Fort—"approximately one-half attended in automobile.…More than 8,000 automobiles were parked in the park July 4. Every attraction and concession reported a record business for the last month." But the midway was cleared that same year to be used for a children's playground.

Tokio Gardens

Managed by Crescent Amusement and opened in 1924, Tokio Gardens was a large, enclosed dance pavilion decorated as a Japanese garden. Said to be one of the finest dancing venues in the area, it reportedly attracted as many as one thousand couples and two thousand spectators per night

Johnny Bayersdorffer's Jazz Band (Martin Abraham, bass and sousaphone; Leo Adde, drums; Tom Brown, trombone and saxophone; and Bayersdoffer, trombone and violin) was the house orchestra. During the first year, Brownlee's Famous Orchestra (Joe Bonano, cornet; Al Guilbeau, banjo; Joe Loyocano, trombone; Milton Monroe, singer; Harry Shields, saxophone and clarinet; and Norman Brownlee, pianist) also entertained at the garden.

Professor D. Eddie Morton, the director of dancing, often gave demonstrations and lessons while keeping an eye out for any lewd or suggestive movements. Morton may have introduced New Orleanians to the Argentine tango and demonstrated the Flea Hop, the Hesitation Waltz and the One-Step. He formed a Golden Club "for middle-aged and older couples of the city who are interested in better dancing." The Haines-Morton School of Dancing sometimes entertained the crowd with as many as forty dancers. Morton organized themed dance parties and contests. In 1924 alone, he organized a barn dance with exhibition dancers and $200 in prizes (reportedly, three thousand attended), as well as a Bobbed Hair Contest (in conjunction with a Big-Baby Dance). Twelve barbers served as judges to award silver hairbrushes to the ladies exhibiting the most efficient, coquettish and attractive coifs. A pair of silver shears was presented to the barbers who created them. Prizes totaling $200 were also awarded for the best big baby costume, the biggest babies and the best big baby dancers. (Admittance was free to those in costume.) A Flapper Night was held, with prizes for the prettiest, the fattest, the littlest, the tallest and the slenderest flappers. On Tokio Nite, free admission was given for those in costume. The night featured complimentary hot or iced Tokay Tea, souvenirs and novelties imported from Japan and China and $200 in prizes for the best costumes and dancers. A dance tournament was held, with silver loving cups for the winners. There was Department Store Dancing, whereby local stores were assigned designated nights for the entertainment of their employees and friends. Finally, there was Mardi Gras Night, with $100 in prizes for the best maskers, comedy costumes and fancy costumes, as well as for the best masking clubs—all in costume were admitted for free.

In 1925, the Tokio Gardens was moved to the redecorated Tranchina's, where the dance floor was enlarged. For the season opening, Bayersdoffer's Tokio Dance Orchestra and Schilling's Society Serenaders performed. The year included the offering of season tickets, Monday Ladies' Nights (free admittance), Fridays Gentlemen's Nights (men got in for free), prizes for girls dressed as boys and boys as girls, a Japanese party and a minstrel show. In 1926, this short-lived early jazz venue was taken over for use as a dance pavilion for picnickers, accommodating as many as 1,600 people.

The End

Among the last performances at Spanish Fort were Jack Payne's 1926 110-foot dive into 4 feet of water and Galen Gotch the strongman, who allowed an eight-ton truck to be driven over him, could tear three decks of cards in half and allowed himself to be beaten with an iron bar. Spectacular fireworks displays, such as re-creations of the Burning of Rome, the Chicago Fire and a Japan earthquake were curtain calls. But not before a new Custer Car miniature auto speedway was added.

On April 1, 1926, the *Times-Picayune* reported that NOPSI had announced that the last season opening would occur on Easter Sunday. The Orleans Levee Board had demanded that the wharf be demolished and that swimming be prohibited: "next year Spanish Fort will be a part of the great [$27 million] residential and park project being fostered by the levee board.…Incidentally Spanish Fort is the place to go now to see the first of the lakefront development work. Just above the fort ten score of land already have been made by the dredges and acre after acre will be made until the project is completed." At the end of the summer season, the rail

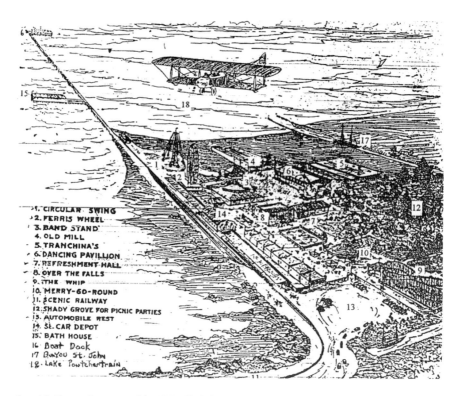

1. CIRCULAR SWING
2. FERRIS WHEEL
3. BAND STAND
4. OLD MILL
5. TRANCHINA'S
6. DANCING PAVILLION
7. REFRESHMENT HALL
8. OVER THE FALLS
9. THE WHIP
10. MERRY-GO-ROUND
11. SCENIC RAILWAY
12. SHADY GROVE FOR PICNIC PARTIES
13. AUTOMOBILE REST
14. St. CAR DEPOT
15. BATH HOUSE
16. Boat Dock
17. Bayou St. John
18. Lake Pontchartrain

Spanish Fort as it appeared in 1927. *BasinStreet.com.*

lines stopped running. Tranchina's had been demolished. The games were removed and the booths demolished. A restaurant and soft drink concessions remained, as did many of the rides.

The April 27, 1926 *New Orleans States* newspaper reported, "Next year Spanish Fort will be 2,000 feet off the lake, and will be covered with mud. The dredges are at work, and mud is being pumped into the lake." On a brighter note, as the land was building up, a sandy beach was taking shape, and despite the prohibition, it became very popular for swimming. Hot dog and soft-drink stands popped up willy-nilly. Thousands of people flocked there, parking their cars along the temporary beach.

PONTCHARTRAIN BEACH AT SPANISH FORT

The original Pontchartrain Beach opened on June 30, 1928, on the newly reclaimed land east of the mouth of Bayou St. John. It was operated by the

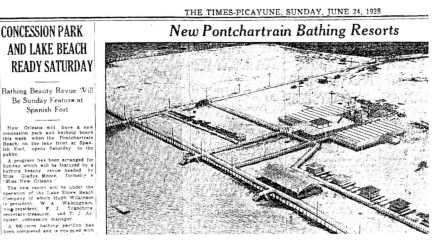

THE TIMES-PICAYUNE, SUNDAY, JUNE 24, 1928

CONCESSION PARK AND LAKE BEACH READY SATURDAY

New Pontchartrain Bathing Resorts

Bathing Beauty Revue Will Be Sunday Feature at Spanish Fort

New Orleans will have a new concession park and bathing beach this week when the Pontchartrain Beach, on the lake front at Spanish Fort, opens Saturday to the public.

A program has been arranged for Sunday which will be featured by a bathing beauty revue headed by Miss Gladys Moore, formerly a "Miss New Orleans."

The new resort will be under the operation of the Lake Shore Beach Company of which Hugh Wilkinson is president; W. A. Walsingham, vice-president; F. J. Tranchina, secretary-treasurer, and T. J. Arculeer, concession manager.

A 600-room bathing pavilion has been completed and is equipped with

Report of the opening of the "New Pontchartrain Bathing Resorts," June 24, 1928. Times-Picayune.

Lake Shore Beach Company, which had built a six-hundred-room bathing pavilion furnished with hair dryers and bathing suits for rent. Concession buildings were still under construction, and admission to the park was free.

A formal opening on July 1 included a beauty contest and a demonstration of aerial warfare and air stunts, ending with a fireworks display. The new facility had twenty-three buildings, including beauty parlors with maids, a casino, a pavilion and food and drink stands under the management of Felix Tranchina (of old Spanish Fort fame) and T.H. Arculeer (who would later operate Lincoln Beach). Admission was free, and in the lake were chutes and a waterwheel.

The following year, the park was enlarged, improved and billed as the "South's Greatest Playground." A "Miracle Music" machine (known as an auditorium orthophonic horn—a loudspeaker used in movie houses and amusement parks to blast Victor Talking Machine record players across wide expanses) was added so that the music "can be heard for miles and miles." In addition, one thousand new lockers were provided in a new bathhouse. Daredevil Rene Muntz delighted the crowd by jumping from an airplane into the lake near the brand-new sand beach, which was one-half mile long and 250 feet deep from the shore. Also new in 1919 were a 2,500-foot roller coaster, a Walking Charlie (manikins weaving along a track with tin cans atop their heads awaiting patrons to knock the cans down) and the Tumble Bug steel amusement ride (later moved to the second Pontchartrain Beach at Milneburg). John Batt's Playland Corporation operated the rides.

An open-air dance hall was under construction, and parking was improved by using the old Spanish Fort park for this purpose. There were daily concerts and beauty contests—local girl Dorothy Dell Goff won the Miss American Legion title at the beach in 1929, went on to win Miss Universe the following year and made four Hollywood films (including *Little Miss Marker*) before she died tragically at age nineteen in a car crash.

The *Wild Cat*, a 3,560-foot scenic railway / roller coaster, was added in 1930. The 1931 season opened with much fanfare, and the stepped seawall was completed from Milneburg. Now there was a mini-railroad and a seaplane along with the old Spanish Fort rides, the Whip, Caterpillar and Aeroplanes. Local products available at the resort included Jacob's Candies, Jackson Brew and Jackson Root Beer. Local girl Dorothy Slaton/ Lambour (later "Lamour") was crowned the first Miss New Orleans in 1931 at this "Coney Island of the South" before becoming a movie star. Pontchartrain Beach would remain the venue for Miss New Orleans contests for years to come.

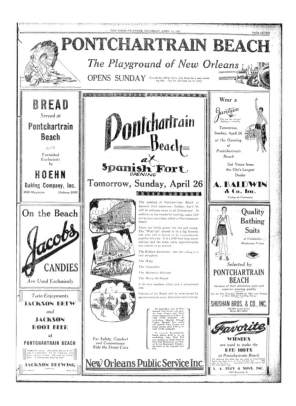

On Sunday, April 26, 1931, the New Pontchartrain Beach at Spanish Fort officially opened. Times-Picayune.

The Water Wedding

Arguably one of the most amusing events to take place here was the July 8, 1931 "Water Wedding" uniting Alice Louis Ensminger, daughter of Percy Ensminger, and Morris Delatte. The couple was chosen from among many who responded to a *Times-Picayune* advertisement.

To the accompaniment of Harry Mendelson's Concert Band playing Felix Mendelssohn's "Wedding March," the couple and bridal party walked down the boardwalk in bathing suits and into waist-high lake water in front of the Casino and stood before an improvised altar. Judge W. Alexander Bahns presided over the ceremony while floating in a boat. Numa Jones served as best man. In lieu of rice, water was tossed on the couple, ruining the bride's permanent wave.

After the "I do's," they donned traditional wedding dress and tuxedo to cut a huge wedding cake, which was distributed to the crowd (reportedly thirty thousand attendees who had snarled traffic for hours before and after). The bride then tossed her bouquet to the lucky lady who might be next year's Water Wedding bride (she wasn't), and the wedding party sped away

After much local hype and support from local businesses, New Orleans's first "Water Wedding" united Alice Louis Ensminger and Morris Delatte, 'til death did they part. Times-Picayune.

for supper at the Club Forest on Jefferson Highway and the married couple lived happily ever after.

Everything needed for the wedding (from bridal and formal wear to the bridal supper) and wedding gifts were donated by local businesses. Gifts were on display in the Casino. They included a complete bedroom suite and a ton of coal.

Changes

On October 16, 1932, the Spanish Fort streetcar made its last run to Lake Pontchartrain. A bus replaced it. The Orleans Levee Board took possession of the amusement park in 1933 when the lessee, Lake Shore Beach Corporation, fell $11,900 in arrears. Harry J. Batt (proprietor James Batt's son) took over as secretary-treasurer of the family's Playland Corporation (owner of the rides) and secured the lease, stating that he had already invested $70,000 at the park.

In 1934, Regal Beer became the "Official Beer of Pontchartrain Beach." A 1935 renovation resulted in a "modern colors scheme" of red, white, blue and yellow. "Streets of Paris," a new attraction modeled after one at the Chicago World's Fair, offered a boardwalk café with a French theme. Parking was added for one thousand cars. Aerial and vaudeville acts, including the Flying Lavans, were the major forms of entertainment.

A second Water Wedding was celebrated, uniting Elsie Hagner and Pontchartrain Beach lifeguard Merlin Andrews on August 12, 1936. Park promoters said they chose this couple because he had saved her from drowning five years prior. And he had wooed her at the beach, where there was now a Loop-a-Plane ride, the Hooded Daredevils trapeze artists, the Three Aces flying ring and stunt high-wire pyramid cyclists Blondin-Rellims riding from fifty feet above.

Girl high-diver Bee Kyle's backward somersault from one hundred feet above into a flaming six-foot-deep tank only fifteen feet wide was a highlight of the park's tenth season in 1937. A contest was held to find the person possessing the most freckles; it was judged by former *Our Gang* actor Jack "Freckles" Ray. During this summer session, cyclist Oscar (now billed as "Loop") Babcock returned to thrill the throngs.

In 1938, a jitterbug dance contest was a fun event, but the park was scheduled to be demolished by the levee board after September of that year to make way for parks and homesites in a never-to-be-realized Lake Air development. Pontchartrain Beach was moving to a site three times larger on reclaimed land in front of what used to be Milneburg. The sand beach there had yet to be formed, but the new park would open in Milneburg in 1939. The sand beach of the original Pontchartrain Beach would be called, for generations afterward, the "Old Beach," and it's a good bet that not many youngsters knew why.

In 1937, NOPSI sold its Spanish Fort property to the Orleans Levee Board for $150,000. The levee board swapped it with City Park for land it planned for building new subdivisions. The immediate fort area is now owned by City Park.

2

MILNEBURG

Milneburg is the truly republican stamping-ground, where all classes congregate and where each moves in its own particular orbit…on a Sunday afternoon a perfect rainbow of colors.
—Daily Picayune, *June 12, 1839*

Scottish native Alexander Milne made his fortune in New Orleans in the brick-making business that boomed after the Great Fire of 1788 and a subsequent destructive blaze in 1794. He came to own twenty-two miles along the Pontchartrain shoreline from Jefferson Parish to the Rigolets—one and a half miles back from the lake. When he died in 1838, he bequeathed a portion of his landholdings for the establishment of an orphanage for boys and another for girls in the town he had established around 1830, one and one-fourth miles east of Bayou St. John. Old-time New Orleanians most often called it "Milenburg."

In 1830, the Pontchartrain Railroad was chartered (buying its right-of-way from Milne) to establish a port and railroad terminus and with the right to develop a harbor, pier and warehouse. The harbor's trestle/wharf extended some one and a half miles into the lake for trains to connect directly to steamboats, which would ply to Mobile and then farther along the Gulf Coast.

In 1831, Port Pontchartrain was established by the U.S. Congress. The Pontchartrain Railroad initiated service to the city levee at Elysian

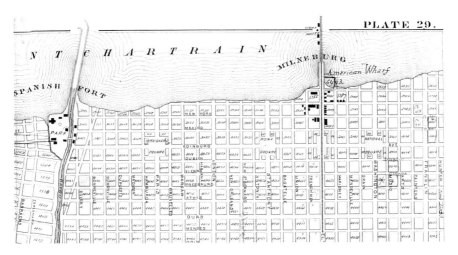

Before land reclamation, the port town of Milneburg hugged the shoreline, approximately two miles east of Spanish Fort. Its lighthouse stood far out in the lake. *Author's collection.*

Fields Avenue (five to six cars pulled by horses) on April 23, 1831—an approximate five-and-a-half-mile journey. The resort did not get off to a good start; the railroad built an eighty-foot bathhouse that was soon afterward demolished by a hurricane that brought lake waters as far as Dauphine Street.

Although well known for its beautiful gardens, most of the structures at Milneburg were built over the lake on pilings, many of them connected to one another by wooden walkways or to the train wharf. Of the hundreds of camps, clubs, restaurants and joints built over the water, only a few of the major attractions were on solid ground: the Washington Hotel, Gardens and Dance Pavilion on the western side of the wharf; Boudro's Restaurant and Gardens, Miguel's Phoenix House and the Magnolia Pleasure Club to the east. The Arch House was built over the railroad tracks.

From these humble beginnings, the town of Milneburg grew to become, for a time, the finest and most popular resort along Lake Pontchartrain. While Milneburg never included an amusement park, it did provide entertainment of many sorts. Filled with rowdies and families, pistol shooting and domino games, picnics and banquets, billiard parlors and ten-pin alleys, dancing and gambling, orchestras and bands, it was a noted birthplace of jazz.

Pontchartrain Railroad

In 1831, the railroad built the Lake House hotel and tavern on an 830-foot pier. The following year, the company constructed three bathhouses, one exclusively "for the colored population" on the wharf of the newly built Washington Hotel. During the late 1830s, there was Armstrong's Hotel, which also offered food and drink, and Lake Porter House, a bottling business producing port and ale operated by A. Loomis. In complement with the railroad, the excursion steamer *Mazeppa* was traveling to Mandeville and the *Giraffe* to Mobile in 1839.

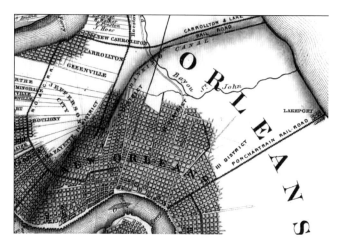

A section of B.M. Norman's 1858 chart of the lower Mississippi River shows the little town of Milneburg named "Lakeport." It has also been known as Port Pontchartrain and Lake End. *Author's collection.*

"Ponchartrain Railroad 5 mile line from Elysian Fields Street to the Shore of Lake Ponchartrain at Milneburg" is written on this undated engraving. *Louisiana State Library.*

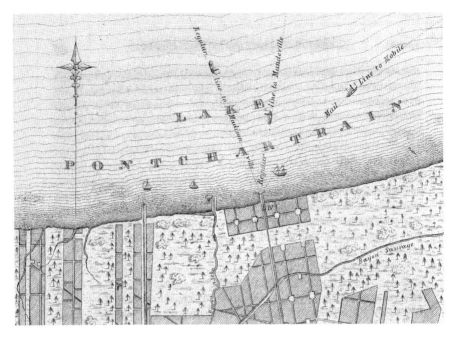

Milneburg developed into a thriving port handling goods shipped to and from Mandeville, Madisonville, Mobile and beyond. *Author's collection.*

It was the first railroad in Louisiana and the second chartered railroad in the United States. It was the first to use a loading system whereby the car beds were at the same level as the loading platform. An empty boxcar served as a jail to hold and haul troublemakers to the New Orleans prison. There were no turnabouts, so the train ran in reverse from town and forward from Milneburg.

BOUDRO'S RESTAURANT

Lucien Boudro opened a restaurant in Milneburg around 1832. In the 1840s, he had a restaurant and hotel at West End, but in 1849, he opened a new establishment in Milneburg at the railroad terminus in "The Arc of Triomphe" (also known as the Arch House; see later in this chapter), serving the finest food, wine, liquor and cordials amid lush gardens filled with oak, magnolia and orange trees, as well as flower beds and sweet olive, rose, jasmine and camellia bushes.

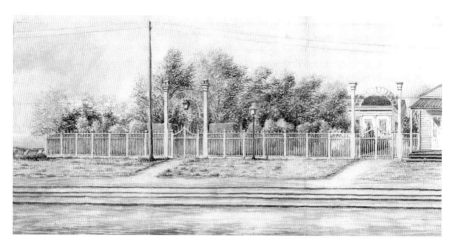

Boudro's restaurant in Milenburg by an unknown artist. *Historic New Orleans Collection.*

William Makepeace Thackeray dined at Boudro's Garden (later Mr. and Mrs. Francis Carrau's Washington Garden) on March 28, 1856. Lucien also cooked for Jenny Lind, the Pontalbas and the Marignys. He died in 1867 at the age of fifty-seven as one of the most celebrated chefs in the city. But his name and restaurant lived on for years after.

In 1878, Boudro's was given an "overhaul…now in 1st class condition," reported proprietors Arthur Jary and Alex Hauss. An Italian Day was celebrated in 1889 at Boudro's Garden with fireworks, a ball in the dance hall and an Italian Beneficial Society banquet at the Washington Hotel, where Jean Trisconi cooked an Italian repast.

In 1901, a storm swept away even the foundation of Boudro's Garden and Pleasure Hall, then owned by Louis A. Chapotel. The dance hall was huge, four hundred by five hundred feet. Sometime before 1911, it was purchased by Mr. and Mrs. Francois Carrau, who gave it their name. The property remained in their family until the reclamation project wiped it out.

WASHINGTON HOTEL

A native of England, Henry Bax (later at the Lake House in West End) managed this luxurious establishment, which was owned by the railroad in 1832. A highlight of the opening year was a mile-high balloon ascension at the hotel whereby a flag-holding patriotic statuette wafted down from the heavens. In 1841, August Brouant opened a new restaurant here, but the following year, a Mr. Lehmann was in charge of the hotel and announcing weekly Sunday orchestra concerts followed by balls. The place was taken over by C.L. Bell (1844), then a Mr. Kennedy (1849), followed by Jule Cource, then Edward Denechaud (1869).

An 1869 description of the Washington Hotel and grounds tells us of a large gate to a garden surrounding a two-story building. Upstairs was reserved for dining. Downstairs was a barroom, saloon and garden with tables for refreshments, drinks and amusements and an adjoining pavilion built in 1860 by John Trisconi, who managed the downstairs properties. Denechaud and Trosconi became famous for their businesses here, and they later owned others.

By 1876, Denechaud had moved out to West End, and the Washington was closed. Declining due to neglect by the railroad and competition with Spanish Fort and West End, by 1878, train service was cut back from departures every thirty minutes to every sixty minutes, a mere three or four trips per day. The *Smokey Mary* did stop at the vacant Washington Hotel but ceased service down to the end of the wharf, where a quarter-mile stretch of restaurants, camps, boathouses and a "great shed" were located. The shell carriage road from the city was also in disrepair.

In 1880, the hotel was renovated and the grounds improved. E.A. Weeks Esq., for the Southern News Company, took over its management. Miguel Brisolari and Trisconi leased the Washington Hotel, restaurant, garden,

The Milneburg Playground in 1912. *New Orleans Public Library.*

grounds and men's and women's bathhouses in 1882. By 1887, Trisconi was also managing the adjoining new Milneburg Opera House.

In the early 1900s, regattas were headquartered at the hotel, and in 1903, a dance pavilion was attached. In 1911, Washington Gardens was converted into the Milneburg Playground, but the hotel remained open. In 1913, it was used for Catholic masses attended by one hundred or so residents and as many as five hundred visitors in summer months. Father Alex Chasles officiated over an altar made by townsman Ben L. Larmann.

In 1920, the railroad ordered the destruction of the Washington Hotel and dismantled it "to make way for Modern needs." The foundation bricks and timber were used for work in the playground.

Arch House

This tavern actually straddled the railroad tracks on the wharf. An 1839 advertisement reveals that proprietor Thomas Tucker invited young gentlemen for recreation and boarding at his "summer retreat" at Port Ponchartrain and its attached bar room, the Arch Coffee House, for fine spirits. An 1857 fire destroyed the place when it was run by persons named Lopez and Hernandez.

By 1860, a new, enlarged Arch House had been built. An April 23 *New Orleans Daily Crescent* article tells us that "Mr. Leclere (formerly Garzia) is keeper serving courbillon [*sic*], croakers, pompano, soft crabs, and other delicacies, fresh out of the lake and fresh from the city markets….Besides the usual rooms for families and private parties, a large and elegant rear pavilion has been added, where at least three hundred men may seat themselves at table, with the broad lake in front; this being the only restaurant with such an exposure." The reason for the demise of the Arch House is not known, but it is possible that it was destroyed in an 1865 fire.

1840–1850s

In 1841, the railroad initiated fishermen's excursions, which ran from the city daily at 4:00 a.m. The steamboat *Southerner* and steamer *Creole* began running to Bay St. Louis, Pass Christian, Biloxi and Pascagoula in 1842. In the 1840s, the Smack Coffee House and bar and a Ten Pin Alley were for sale by A. Armstrong. A family bathhouse equipped with towels and bathing suits was in operation, and two rowing clubs had formed.

In the 1850s, the Monona and the Pioneer clubs hosted boat races, a very popular spectator sport of the day. In 1855, the current lighthouse was completed. It is now the only vestige of Milneburg still standing in what is now the University of New Orleans Technology Park, the former Pontchartrain Beach.

Miguel's/Phoenix Restaurant

Miguel Brisolari was already a popular chef when he opened his restaurant in Milneburg in 1859. In 1878, the restaurant and saloon was refitted and refurnished. In 1879, John Trisconi partnered with Miguel, and in 1882, Brisolari and Trisconi leased the Washington Hotel. Miguel was hired by the Tranchinas at "The Cottage" in 1888.

1860s–1890s

An 1865 fire that started at the Mobile Oyster Saloon across from the Washington Hotel spread to consume twenty buildings. Destroyed were Boudro's Hotel, Hope House, Miguel's Phoenix restaurant, Fritz Bullinger's and John Earhart's grocery stores. That same year, the newly decommissioned former USS *Osceola* side-wheel Union navy gunboat began transporting goods and people to the Pascagoula River in Mississippi. The following year, the elegant steamer *Mary* of the Morgan steamship line began its daily route through the Rigolets to Mobile Bay, complete with a gentlemen's saloon, ladies' saloon, sleeping accommodations for 170 passengers, a spacious dining room, eighty sleeping berths, staterooms and a dancing deck. Piloted by Captain Abe Myers, it replaced the steamer *Frances*.

Until the 1870s, Morgan line steamers plied from Milneburg to Galveston, while two new large bathhouses were constructed, two older ones renovated and John Trisconi's Lunch Bowl Saloon and Schneider's restaurant opened. Gas lighting on twenty streetlamps as well as at Denechaud's and Boudro's was installed in 1871 before a fire destroyed

Denechaud's Pavilion, where free concerts with cake and ice cream had been enjoyed.

By 1875, the little town had become a true community, but the railroad company was not maintaining the road to it. An 1877 storm damaged the wharf, putting a temporary halt on the *Camelia* steamer's trips to Mandeville and West End. In 1879, a fire that started near Miguel's destroyed the northeastern section of the town except Boudro's main building near the lake. Also in that year, a road was opened to Spanish Fort by Moses Schwartz's City Park and Lake Railroad, making competition with the Bayou St. John resort more onerous. But by the end of the decade, the Pontchartrain Railroad was back on schedule.

The Louisville and Nashville Railroad acquired the Pontchartrain Railroad in 1880 and ran a telegraph line from the lake to the city. It also built several large bathhouses, took ownership of the Washington Hotel and rebuilt the wharves, railroad pier and steamboat landing. The following year, the railroad company remodeled the hotel, built and extended a new boardwalk a half mile, roofed a portion of the wharf and added a shed for refreshments and a refreshment room near the steamer landing. By 1882, the trains ran every twenty minutes, and entertainment included tightrope walkers, trapeze artists, African American minstrels, pantomime acts and the Kennie & Valdez brass band.

Contestants Max Burgdorf, P. Dale, John Miller and Mike O'Brien competed for a $1,000 purse in a six-day "Walking Match" that began on July 19, 1881. Meanwhile, at West End, four walkers were vying for $500 in a six-day competition. New Orleanians August Bowman, J.J. Johnson and John Rickfert were to each walk 48 hours while professional pedestrienne Madame Dupree of Chicago hoped to beat their combined total of 144 hours in a shorter duration. Pedestrianism, walking races held on tracks, was a popular competitive sport that attracted many fans prior to the mid-1880s.

Aeronautic professor Zero manned a sixty-by-forty-five-foot balloon to soar high above while hanging from a trapeze bar in 1884, and the Milneburg Opera House presented vaudeville and comedy. Grand concerts by Professor Alois Schindler's Orchestra, variety shows and fireworks displays filled the bill in 1886.

In 1887, a new opera house was built under the management of Harry Webber, with Schindler as the musical director. The very popular musical burlesque *The Mikado of New Orleans* satirized topics of local interest and included a fifty-girl choir. The following year, a storm washed away the shed east of the wharf as well as the largest two bathhouses, leaving only

This 1895 sketch from the *New Orleans Mascot* newspaper illustrates behavior along the shore between Spanish Fort and Milneburg, which was "exciting comment." New Orleans Mascot.

one remaining on the western side. From the late 1880s to the mid-90s, shooting matches were popular events.

By the mid-1890s, thirty new private clubs and camps had sprouted up along the wharf—places for friends and family to picnic and party, with bands hired for entertainment and dancing. But the commercial venues were growing thinner, and the number of people riding out to Milneburg was waning, even though it offered some of the best fishing and bathing on the lakefront. Only a few public bathhouses remained. A regatta was held in 1896.

MOREAU'S AT MILNEBURG

The Moreau family has a long history on Lake Pontchartrain. About 1899, Moreau's restaurant opened in Milneburg and became well known for serving some of the finest renditions of local seafood. Moreau's Hall was a popular venue for private picnics, with dancing and amusements. In 1922, when the reclamation project doomed the town, Charles Moreau's grocery had been in business for fifty-eight years. A July 10, 1949 *Times-Picayune* article pictures the then-still-existing Moreau's Grocery building in juxtaposition to its location in 1928, which verifies that the old place was spared.

1900s

In 1900, a shell road ran along what is now Frenchmen/Vermillion Streets parallel to and slightly west of Elysian Fields. Some six hundred vehicles would ride out to Milneburg on Sundays to the camps and clubhouses, which were now lining the shore on either side of Milneburg.

In the early 1900s, even more private and club camps sprang up. In 1900 alone, new additions included the Palmetto camp, East End Club, Lakeview Cottage and the Umback Sporting Club. New private camps included O'Mallen's (1906), Leo Social Club (1907), Hausemann Club, Our Club, Fry's Clubhouse, Lakeview Sunset, Pelican Clubhouse and Happy Day Camp (1908). Some good examples of how these camps were enjoyed are a party at Annex Cottage in 1909, with dancing to the Imperial Orchestra; a picnic at Camp Dexter, with Kling's Band and bathing, boating, sailing, then breakfast, a swimming contest, a cakewalk, a rowing race and dinner.

The Milneburg Light in 1906. *Author's collection.*

A view from the Milneburg light in the early 1900s. Times-Picayune.

An August 1901 storm resulted in severe flooding of camps and bathhouses. The railroad trestle and wharf were washed away and its shed destroyed. All camps that survived were damaged. Eight inches of water seeped into Moreau's, and Boudro's Garden was left covered with debris and uprooted plants and trees. The iron-hulled, 106-foot-long steamer *Neptune*, which was docked on the wharf, was broken to pieces. Remains of all these structures washed to shore and covered yards in the town.

Another storm in 1904 left the new wharf underwater and Moreau's grocery (one thousand feet from shore) flooded. Then a fire destroyed eight hundred feet of wharf, including the New Camelia's landing. The conflagration started at Moreau's saloon on the right side of the track—it burned to the ground. Townspeople formed a bucket brigade and chopped the wharf with axes near shore to prevent the spread of flames. Moreau's restaurant (left side of the track) was damaged. The following year, another fire destroyed the Laura B and American Eagle cottages.

Quarrella's

John Quarella's big over-the-water dancing pavilion was opened midway down the main pier around 1906. He also owned a restaurant, a barroom, a cabaret, a sweet shop, a grocery, a butcher stand and several camps that he rented off his own three-hundred-foot pier. A picnic in those days was an all-day party, consisting of lunch, games, competitions, bands hired for entertainment and dancing, swimming, fishing, boating, dinner and perhaps even a ball. Quarrella was equipped to handle any of these.

An Italian society banquet was held at Quarrella's Midway restaurant in 1913, attended by three hundred to four hundred, who also used his rear pavilion. By 1914, he was often referred to as the "Mayor of Milneburg," and he volunteered in 1921 to serve as a test case when authorities began cracking down on what they deemed "immoral dancing" in dance halls—he was arrested for allowing such an exhibit to take place in his establishment but argued that the couples were dancing not in a hall, but on his porches.

Jazz musicians who played at Quarrella's venues included (among many others) his brother-in-law Sharkey Bonano, Frank Christian, Charlie Christian, Ernest Giardina, Tony Giardina, Tony Parenti and Tony Sbarbaro.

Left to right, Gennaro "John" Quarrella, his wife, Marie Bonano (sister of jazz great Sharkey Bonano), John's brother Joseph Quarrella and the Midway's bartender, circa 1914. *Marie Bonano.*

John Quarrella died shortly before news of the reclamation/destruction of all he had owned in Milneburg, but his widow remained there in her home with her principal source of income about to be lost.

BOXING AT MILNEBURG

In 1908, former world featherweight champion "Young Corbett II" (William J. Rothwell) was working out at Milneburg with trainer Dave Barry. In (or slightly before) 1914, local lightweight boxer Phil "Philly" Virgets set up a training camp at Milneburg. He considered rowing in the lake as the ideal exercise for conditioning arms and shoulders. His brothers Nick "Stanocola Kid" and featherweight Harry were also boxers. "Young Denny" (Herbert LaCroix), a 145-pound local welterweight, trained at Virgets in 1914. In 1921, Virgets was still active at Milneburg.

In 1915, boxers Frankie Russell (Frank Merenda)—a lightweight who owned a camp he used for training—and Jack Doyle and featherweight Tango "Kid" Bronson, along with Russell's trainer Tony Pace and Charles "Babe" White, were arrested at Quarrella's pavilion. They were charged with being dangerous and suspicious characters who had pickpocketed watches. They were also charged with stealing jewelry and clothing from Milneburg bathhouses. Bantamweight boxer "One-Punch" Hogan (Henry Galliano) turned himself in to the authorities later the same night after finishing/losing a fifteen-round prizefight at the Tulane Club arena. The prior Saturday, Milneburg saloon propietor Robert Virgets (brother of "Philly" Virgets) noticed that his watch was gone from his pocket and suspected that one of the Russell group had taken it. He spoke with Russell about this, and his watch was returned. The boxers had spent most of the summer at Russell's camp, presumably in training. In 1916, the King Do-Do Social Club used Emile Marquez's camp as its headquarters (*King DoDo* was a musical comedy popular in the early 1900s). This camp had been Russell's training headquarters.

In 1916, Hogan was training at the Milneburg Club, sparring daily with featherweights Paul "Battling" Barrere, Michael "Kid" Murphy and Dutch Gardner. That same year, renowned restaurateur Hippolyte Begue cooked stingray with bordelaise and black butter sauce at lightweight Joe "Baker Boy" Mandot's camp for Joe's friends.

1910s–1920s

In 1911, the private Capitol Club was built on Franklin Avenue at the lake. Club owners formed a co-op of sorts to build a new boardwalk from the railroad tracks to Franklin Avenue. It would be fronted by a ten-foot-high bulkhead and run about one mile long and five to ten feet wide and would reach hundreds of camps.

Hickmeck's Club was built in 1913. The club camp was located opposite Quarrella's pavilion. Finley's Dance Hall and Fahey & Gahagen's saloon were hopping, but the Milneburg Civic Improvement Association met to organize its own "policing" of rowdies after newspaper reports of trouble began affecting some businesses.

Other new private camps were the Joy Camp, Happy Cottage, Obeiling Camp and Happy B., all built in 1914. That year, the steamer *Hanover* began excursion trips to Spanish Fort, Mandeville and Madisonville. A fire consumed Moreau's Dance Hall (on the west side of the wharf) and one hundred feet of wharf, along with Moreau's Restaurant on the east side. Lighthouse keeper Margaret Norvell's home was in peril, as the roof of the adjoining boathouse had also caught fire. (Also residing there were her daughter Lillian and Mrs. Bob Lamson.) Once again, townspeople organized a bucket brigade and used water from the train's steam boiler to quell the flames. In 1915, another fire destroyed Moreau's Bathhouse and part of the wharf.

In 1915, the first policewoman in New Orleans went on duty in Milneburg. Alice Monahan, in an effort to preserve respectability in Milneburg, banned men from wearing pajamas and women from donning "Bungalow Aprons" (at the center of the accompanying image, from Eaton's 1920 catalog) on piers. These "aprons" were short enough to reveal far above the knees of

A Bungalow Apron (top center) as seen in Eaton's 1920 catalogue. *Author's collection.*

any woman when reaching overhead. Officer Monahan also put an end to "promiscuous bathing."

Despite Officer Monahan's efforts, in 1921, all dance halls were shut down as being "undesirable." This didn't keep them from operating under cover. By 1926, Columbia and America Streets along the shore had mostly washed away over the years, leaving the property of M.L. Carrau (formerly Boudro's) very near the lake waters. It mattered not, because this land would be covered and set blocks back from the new shoreline by the impending reclamation project. But Paradise Gardens bar and restaurant, as well as Manuel's Pavilion, were still in operation in 1927 when Tony Denier's Humpty Dumpty the clown pantomime was a popular attraction.

The town of Milneburg's end had come. Trucks carrying belongings and salvaged building materials from homes, camps and businesses were familiar sights around the city in 1928. "For sale" ads in local newspaper classified sections offered, for example, "Foster's Restaurant, good lumber, doors, iron bed, cistern, large bar and fixtures." In 1929, the lighthouse was deactivated.

In 1928, the dredges were at Milneburg to begin expanding the shoreline. *New Orleans Public Library.*

Jazz

What went on at West End and Spanish Fort was regulated by the railroad companies that owned them. Milneburg and Bucktown were entirely more freewheeling, with camps sprouting up almost haphazardly. Where there were camps to "picnic" (party) in, there were usually also bands hired cheaply for entertainment and dancing. Old-timers described battles of the bands ("bucking" and/or "cutting contests"), where camps were in such near proximity to one another that one band would try to "outplay" the other. In this way, many musicians were exposed to new sounds, which they tried to emulate, improve upon and then mold into something entirely their own—something new. And so Milneburg was, of all the lakeside resorts, the most important seedbed for what would become known as jazz.

Louis Armstrong played there as a member of the Colored Waifs Home for Boys Band, which also played gigs at Little Woods. To name just of few of the many early jazz venues at Milneburg, there was the Bombela, Fahey & Gahagan's, the Hazel Club, the Hilda Club, the Little Brown Jug, the Little Eva Camp, the Log Cabin, Manuel's Pavilion, the Owl Club, Sam's Camp, Quarrella's and many other public and private camps and clubs.

The following list of jazz musicians who performed at Milneburg is long but entirely incomplete: Albert Artiques, Achille Baquet, Paul Barbarin, Danny Barker, Emile Barnes, Sidney Bechet, Buddy Bolden, Sharkey Bonano, Al Brown, Tom Brown, Abbie Brunies, George Brunies, Merrit Brunies, Richard Brunies, Jack Carey, Papa Celestin, Charlie Christian, Emile Christian, Frank Christian, Kid Clayton, Octave Crosby, Eddie Earmann, Abbey "Chinee" Foster, Willie Foster, Manny Gabriel, Ernest Giardina, Tony Giardina, Eddie "Ti Boy" Gilmore, Avery "Kid" Howard, Armand Hug, Willie Humphrey, Yank Johnson, Papa John Joseph, Chris Kelly, Freddie Keppard, Louis Keppard, Nick LaRocca, Arnold Loyacano, Joe Loyacano, Punch Miller, Andrew Morgan, Sam Morgan, Big Eye Louis Nelson, Joe Oliver, Kid Ory, Dave Oxley, Tony Parenti, Santo Pecora, Manuel Perez, George Peterson, Buddy Petit, Alphonse Picou, Armand Piron, Johnny Provenzano, Alexis Richard, Eddie Richardson, Emanuel Salyes, Willie Santiago, Tony Sbarbaro, Buddy Schilling, Happy Schilling, Harry Shannon, Kid Thomas, Harrison Verret, Albert Walters, Sonny White and Alfred Williams

After news of the encroaching land reclamation project was announced, New Orleans Rhythm Kings member Jelly Roll Morton (Ferdinand Joseph LaMothe), Paul Mares and Leon Rappolo paid homage to the doomed "cradle of jazz" where they had played. They named their tune "Milenburg Joys" (based on the pronunciation of the town by locals at the time). They recorded it in 1923 and played it around the country.

THE TOWN

Among the southshore resorts, only Bucktown and Milneburg functioned as true "towns" (though Bucktown/East End was never incorporated as such). After being plotted by Milne, one of the earliest community projects was the construction of a schoolhouse in 1849. Other examples of residents looking out for one another include the following situations.

When Joseph "Crab Joe" Gonzales, a well-known fisherman and watchman for the camps, died in 1911, neighbors paid for his burial and cared for his beloved dog, Beefsteak.

The town hired a kindergarten teacher in 1913 for the twenty-five children who used the community playground and funded Sunday programs for the young children.

When steamboat captain William "Safety Bill" Willis took ill in 1914, he was brought to the lightkeeper's home (adjacent to the lighthouse), where Margaret "Madge" Ruth Norvell (who would later serve as the keeper of the West End/New Basin Light) attended to his needs until he died. That same year, Norvell's daughter Lillian organized a picnic for orphans at the playground and procured donated food, drinks and prizes for them. Mr and Mrs. Moreau allowed their restaurant to be used for lunch and freely opened their bathhouse for the children's use. The steamer *Hanover* offered them free boat rides. After peanut hunts and games, J.F. Fahey offered his pavilion at the end of the pier, where music for dancing was provided by pianist Arnold Habbe.

Shortly before the public became aware of Milneburg's impending doom, in 1921, St. Rita's Mission Church was dedicated for worship for the 250 Catholics in fifty families. The framed structure sat one block from the rail station.

In 1921, Norvell's son Thomas wrote a letter to the editor decrying the lack of train service (as the *Smokey Mary* seldom ran on any schedule at that time) and the terrible condition of the auto road to Milneburg. He feared for the safety of residents who might need quick access to New Orleans in the event of a medical emergency and the inability of firetrucks from the city to make their way to the lake if a major fire occurred in Milneburg.

THE END

In 1922, there were 1,600 residents in Milneburg. Many owned nothing but their camp and/or business and the contents found within—the land was owned by the City of New Orleans. When residents learned of plans for the land reclamation and the forced move of camps, homes, churches, businesses and schools, they were devastated. For example, Mr. and Mrs. Kopp, who had settled in 1851, would lose their home and fishing boat rental business, while Edward Bell, who had been a fruit and vegetable purveyor for twenty-five years, would have no place to do business. Like some other structures, Sportsmen's Rest camp was spared but only by barging it to another location (probably the Hayne Boulevard/Little Woods area).

A field office for the reclamation project was set up in the Milneburg lighthouse area. On July 8, 1930, work began at 7:00 a.m. The work contract called for five hundred days to completion at a cost of $1.9 million for the five-and-a-half-mile-long seawall with a total cost, including the land-building, of $23 million.

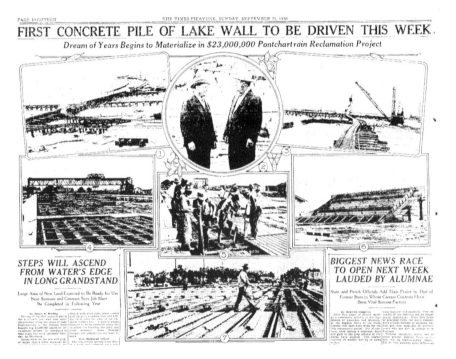

In September 1930, seawall construction began as the first pilings were driven at Milneburg, which served as a base of operations for casting yards, offices, engineers, et cetera. Times-Picayune.

On Tuesday, March 15, 1932, the Pontchartrain Railroad's *Smokey Mary* made its way, for the last time, from the city to the lake. Engineer John H. Galivan, who ran the train seven times a day for most of his thirty-two years on the rails, pushed three coaches and a baggage car to the lake. The train was jammed with New Orleanians from all walks of life who had come out for one last ride after one hundred years in service. This was in contrast to the usual run during the final years, when the train was used primarily to transport goods used for the land building. Meanwhile, and since 1928, Pontchartrain Beach was still operating back at Spanish Fort. That, too, would change.

Pontchartrain Beach at Milneburg

You'll never make it. You put too much money into this.
—Pontchartrain Beach proprietor John W. Batt to his son regarding moving the amusement park from Bayou St. John to Milneburg in 1939. Mr. Batt died shortly after, and his son Harry J. Batt kept the place going for forty-five more years.

In 1938, the new beach in front of what had been the town of Milneburg had a boardwalk and a few vendors with penny and nickel attractions. When Harry Batt moved Pontchartrain Beach to the new fifty-acre site, he took the ten-year-old "Bug" (among other rides) with him. The old steel machine was still there when the park closed, as were other antique curios in the Penny Arcade. The long-lived term *Gay Midway* was first used during this year.

At the new Pontchartrain Beach, Batt's Playland Amusements owned and operated the rides and concessions (a $500,000 investment); the levee board owned the land and maintained it, the sand beach and the bathhouses. The rides were housed in a large air-conditioned building. A concrete midway (which was longer than the beach at that time) separated the park from the sand beach

From west to east were: the air-conditioned, 60-by-260-foot steel ride building designed to house the Scooter, Flying Horses and a newer version of the Bug; the Penny Arcade, which even then was loaded with antique devices—palm readers, rifles, strength testers and dozens more; the Octopus ride (later converted into the Monster); stainless-steel food concession booths; a shelter house; the four-hundred-seat Spanish Gardens, planted with palms and furnished with an orchestra; the main entrance at Elysian Field; the

Milneburg Light; the Zephyr, the air-conditioned Tango Palace; Ride 'N' Laff ride; Shooting Gallery; the Bug; the futuristic Rocket Ship ride; and the Photomatic, producing instant framed photos at the drop of a coin.

THE ZEPHYR

On April 23, 1939, the Zephyr first whisked New Orleanians into the sky along its 2,800-foot winding path around the park. It was 80 feet high and able to reach speeds of ninety or more miles per hour (another source says fifty), and it was hoisted up the first rise powered by an electrically driven chain (click, click, click) then sped around on its under-two-minute route powered by gravity alone.

The Zephyr's wooden superstructure was designed and built by local engineers and tradesmen and constructed of pine for resiliency. Each car

On June 18, 1939, at Milneburg, the Zephyr first whisked New Orleanians into the sky along its winding path around the park. Times-Picayune.

weighed in at 1,250 pounds, locked to steel tracks by way of four tri-sided wheels that grabbed onto the top, side and bottom of the rails. Car bases were made of oak for strength and their bodies built of poplar for durability.

The design for the station landing/loading house was based on the stainless-steel "silver streak" Zephyr engine car of the Chicago, Burlington and Quincy Railroad, which debuted in 1934 as the first successful Streamline Moderne train in the United States.

THE GREAT WALLENDAS

On Sunday, July 30, 1939, the Great Wallendas high-wire troupe performed one of their famous pyramid formations. Without a net, two aerialists carried two others on a unicycle balanced on a pole between their shoulders. The lake breeze was too gusty for the fourth and fifth members to, as planned, form a higher tier to the formation. However, Frank Wallenda thrilled the crowd by pretending to fall, then caught himself on the wire, only to repeat the antics over again. This was the first performance of an engagement of two shows nightly, three on Sundays.

A crowd on the shorelne in the early 1940s. Times-Picayune.

Soon after, the youngest member of the Wallendas met nineteen-year-old Pontchartrain Beach waitress Marian Mohlman. They fell in love and decided to marry. So they did, on August 10, 1939, at Pontchartrain Beach. Matron of honor Henrietta Wallenda, best man Arthur Wallenda, patriarch Karl Wallenda and the groom, Phillip Kreis (Karl's brother-in-law), dressed in formal wear, formed a bridal procession across the high wire to meet Marian beside a clergyman atop the platform used to access the wire. There, they were united in a religious ceremony. "I've never climbed quite so high," she said. Harry Batt promoted this as a "Wedding on the High Wire… The World's Most Daring Nuptials." The reception was held in the beach's Spanish Garden. The public at large was welcome to make reservations to attend the event, which included dinner and dancing to the tunes of the Garden's house band, Don Manuel Sandi and His Orchestra.

Cockeyed Circus

In 1940, a funhouse opened with moving floors, a mirror maze and figures popping up to startle, surprise and perhaps frighten. An open walkway on the second story, under large lighted lettering that spelled out "Cockeyed

A 1941 glimpse of the Cockeyed Circus, the giant clown head and the Ferris wheel. *Works Progress Administration.*

Circus," allowed those on the midway to view hapless fun lovers strolling though the attraction. It was one employee's job to shoot jets of air under females' skirts, years before Marilyn Monroe created a sensation under a similar circumstance.

The adjacent gigantic, open-mouthed clown head that children were inclined to climb into was added during the early 1940s. A mechanical woman was perched in a window, ceaselessly laughing, bobbing and throwing her arms about to attract attention. The Cockeyed Circus was replaced by Circus Daze, then Adventures in Space and finally the Haunted House.

"The Battle of Pontchartrain Beach"

On August 24, 1941, Higgins Industries's City Park Avenue boat-building plant was officially dedicated. Its sole mission was to produce military craft during World War II. The highlight of the day was a "battle" to capture Pontchartrain Beach. At 3:35 p.m., a seventy-foot torpedo boat left the Municipal Yacht Harbor at West End and was "flour bombed" by a navy plane as it passed near the New Canal lighthouse. At 3:45, a fleet of Higgins landing boats and tank-carrying craft left the harbor for an "attack" on Pontchartrain Beach. At 3:46, planes dive-bombed the torpedo boat near the beach. At 4:00, the boat fleet was "bombed." In turn, they fired parachute flares and created a smokescreen to aid in the landing of other craft. Five minutes later, the boats grounded on the beach. At 4:10, tanks and armored cars were landed while sailors and marines waded from boats to aid them. Captives were taken, and at 4:15, the American flag was raised while "The Star-Spangled Banner" was played on the beach loudspeakers. At 4:30, officials departed for the Southern Yacht Club for a cocktail party and supper. Enlisted men partied at the beach with a seafood dinner and free admission to the rides.

During the war years, Harry Batt was a booster of the war effort and supporter of the military personnel stationed at nearby lakefront bases and facilities. One slogan often used in advertisements was, "Where soldiers and sailors play," and he encouraged them to visit often, with reduced admission fees. He also initiated a policy whereby no beer was sold to servicemen after 11:30 p.m. In 1942, the slogan "Work hard for victory and relax at Pontchartrain Beach" was used in advertising to remind civilians that their efforts were also important in waging the war. In 1943, it was "Work first, then have fun." When gas rationing was strongly imposed in 1944, a streetcar shuttle from town carried folks to the beach.

In 1942, a new bathhouse was built, Maximo the clown was walking the high wire, the Miss New Orleans beauty contestants were accompanied by the tunes of Johnnie Detroit's orchestra and the Beach Terrace restaurant opened. A new giant Ferris wheel was put up in 1943. A 1944 fire in the Penny Arcade ruined much of the antique machinery, and new Scooter Cars and Fly-O-Plane Cars were in place.

In the mid-1940s, the Penny Arcade was rebuilt (1945), Buddy the Wonder Seal performed ("He reads, he talks, he plays") (1946) and patrons were invited to "Laugh with Shorty the Clown at the Cockeyed Circus." Shorty was little person Roy Adkisson, who had a long career in different circuses.

A 1947 expansion to accommodate twenty thousand bathers was funded by $350,000 from the levee board, which also expanded the 1,200-foot-long sand beach to 2,600 feet and deepened it from 80 to 400 feet while raising it 5 feet above mean lake level. A new lifeguard station was added, and Warren Easton Night was one of many events that featured high schools presenting fifteen-minute shows that were broadcast over local radio airwaves. In 1948, Circus Daze replaced the Cockeyed Circus.

Kiddieland, which opened in 1947, surrounded the historic Milneburg / Port Pontchartrain lighthouse. *Alexander Allison.*

Kiddieland opened in 1947 near the Milneburg lighthouse with new miniature replicas of adult rides, including a roller coaster and auto scooter. A new administration building, with a stage simulating a ship deck on top, was built in the center of the park. In 1950, the Whiz Bang was introduced. Kiddieland had been such a hit the prior year that it was expanded to add Sky Fighter and Roto-Whip rides.

In the 1950s, a picnic area with tables and benches was set up under the bathhouse (1951), the "Rita Hayworth Beautiful Legs" contest was held and Jax beer sponsored a fireworks display (1952). The Rock-O-Plane and Roll-O-Plane were added in 1953. The Zephyr Junior was moved from Kiddieland in 1954 to provide more play space. By 1955, there were twenty-two rides, including the new Roto-Jet.

Elvis at the Beach

On September 1, 1955, Elvis Presley performed in the Second Annual Hillbilly Jamboree "Celebrating Red Smith" (the emcee) on radio station WBOK Day. Elvis was described as the "Fireball Star of Records and Famous 'Louisiana Hayride'." On that night, there was also the Miss Hillbilly Dumplin' of 1955 beauty contest (the winner of which was awarded an all-expense-paid weeklong vacation at Gulf Hills Dude Ranch in Ocean Springs, Mississippi). Also on the bill were Mrs. Jimmy Rogers, Jim Reeves, Hillbilly Evans and the Flying La Vals.

Actor Ray "Crash" Corrigan and his bride, Elaine DuPont (of the TV show *The Adventures of Rin Tin Tin*), Art Henry's Dog and Pony Show, a jitterbug contest and the "Ideal Boy and Girl of 1956" contests were held that year. In 1957, the Tammy Blue Jeans beauty contest was held and a huge pool complex composed of swimming, diving and wading pools was opened, as was the new "Around the World in 18 Holes" mini-golf course. Trapeze artists Winnie and Dolly soared one hundred feet above the ground, and a fireworks show depicted life-sized Miss Universe Carol Morris (who was there) and Elvis (who wasn't) playing his guitar and singing.

In 1958, the Beachcomber restaurant opened, but after a legal fracas with the West Coast Don the Beachcomber restaurant (which Batt's restaurant was modeled after), it was renamed Bali Hai the following year. Replacing the Beach Terrace, Bali Hai was an immediate and long-term success, serving Polynesian food and potent exotic drinks (think tiki bowl) surrounded by bamboo-lined walls and furnishings. A favorite prom night venue, it served "South Seas tidbits" until 1975. The Ship Ahoy casual restaurant also opened in 1958. The German-made Wild Maus made its debut in 1959, as did Bumbo the comic balloon clown, who appeared regularly in Kiddieland.

In the early years of the space race, Pontchartrain Beach jumped on the bandwagon by introducing in 1960 Space Wheels, a ninety-foot-tall contraption consisting of four large Ferris wheels spinning around a center axis. The old Cockeyed Circus was converted into Adventures in Space, a walk-through of a simulated missile base ending with a "visit" to another planet. The journey began with a blast-off, then an emergency landing, escape through a black-light cavern and then a forty-fathom dive on a Polaris submarine for a second blast-off and landing on "Astra 4." The trip ended by returning to the midway via the "Saturn Slide" or "Lunar Ladder." The exterior of the old funhouse was modernized and equipped with a radar antenna and rocket missiles. The old clown head was painted green and converted into a Martian. John Pela's popular Captain Mercury of local television fame made an appearance. The Easter Bunny, who made annual visits to the park, was dressed as an astronaut that year and renamed Robot Rabbit. On a more traditional note, Old McDonald's Farm was also introduced in 1960, consisting of live chickens, ducks and rabbits performing stunts to the delight of the people.

Other additions in the 1960s were a new Kiddieland helicopter and Burke's Aristocratic Canines (fourteen trick dogs) in 1961 and the Scrambler and Flying Coaster (a miniature version of the Zephyr) in 1962. A new Ghost Ride replaced a similar, older one, and the Rotor made its debut in 1963. A popular innovation of 1964 was POP (pay-one-price) Days, but attendance fell to all-time lows from 1964 to 1969. The Calypso and Trabant, both from Europe, and the American-made Paratrooper as well as Dancing Fountains (a musical water display) were new in 1964.

The *Smokey Mary* returned in the form of an amusement park train in 1965. It was placed in Kiddieland near the old lighthouse where the Pontchartrain Railroad had made its landing back in the day. In 1966, the Giant Space Wheel replaced the Ferris wheel, which had stood for twenty-five years. There was also a new Space Whirl, where riders stood to have the floor drop below them while they were suspended by centrifugal force. The Sky Diver was also new in '66. In 1967, the Haunted House replaced Adventures in Space, and the giant Martian / clown head was either destroyed or engulfed by an addition to the original structure.

By 1968, the fortieth season, there were twenty-one rides—thirteen full-sized and eight in Kiddieland. That year, the Super Wild Maus was the result of a redesign (higher, longer, additional curves) of the original "for greater thrills," and it became as popular as the Zephyr. Also new in 1968 were the Astro Wheel and Olympic Bobsled. The Zacchini Twins were shot from a cannon ninety feet in the air at seventy-five miles per hour. In 1969, the Zephyr was thirty years old, and the pools were closed due to "poor patronage."

Harry Batt retired in 1970 as president and managing director. Harry Batt Jr. took over as president; his brother John Batt was appointed vice-president. They maintained these positions until the park closed. The Kooky Kastle was new that year, as was the Swiss Sky Ride, its open cars soaring sixty feet in the air along one thousand feet of the midway. The Italian-built Galaxy roller coaster and West German Musik Express were introduced in 1971. The next year, a swimming pool was used for the Dolly and Skipper porpoise show.

The $500,000 Log Flume was built over the mini-golf course in 1974. After having acquired five gibbons in 1972 with the hope to add more animals in the future, the Batts opened the $100,000 Fuzzy Farm Petting Zoo in 1974. Yo Yo Wacky Shack, Mine Shaft Tunnel, the Merlin Rainbow Magic Show and a baby elephant were new in 1975. In 1977, the Monster was converted into a giant insect, and a fire destroyed the Wacky Shack.

The 1,600-foot-long, 80-foot-high, forty-mile-per-hour, $1.3 million Rajun Cajun was opened in 1978 during the park's fiftieth anniversary. On stage was an ongoing Gong Show. "Disco Under the Stars" was featured in 1979 for teens who were too young to enjoy adult discos. Also at the stage was a WNOE-FM Talent Search hosted by D.J. Captain Humble (Hugh Dillard) (replacing the Gong Show). Cinema 180 and Sea Dragon were introduced in 1981, and the Gong Show was revived with Captain Humble again as emcee.

By 1982, there were rumblings heard about Pontchartrain Beach being dismantled to build an exclusive six-hundred-unit condominium project (unit prices starting at $100,000) and upscale shopping area. The rumors were true. Developer Stephen Kapelow had brokered a deal with the Batts (whose lease wasn't set to expire until 1999) and the levee board. In 1983, Pontchartrain Beach closed, with a prospect that it might move to another location. The condo project, along with others in coming years, never evolved. In the end, the University of New Orleans was granted rights to the property, which today holds the Research and Technology Park. Kenner mayor Aaron Broussard arranged for the Zephyr's highest peak and other features to be moved to a park in his city. The Bali Hai remained open for several years after, catering private events.

The senior Harry Batt and his beloved wife, Marguerite, had traveled the world in search of new attractions for "the beach." Well known and respected in the amusement industry, Harry Sr. was a co-director of the 1962 Seattle World's Fair and was active in more local charitable and community endeavors than can be included here. When he passed away on November 5, 1977, at age seventy-four of a heart attack, he was doing what he loved, traveling with Marguerite—this last time in Hong Kong.

3

NEW ORLEANS EAST

New Orleans East runs from Seabrook at the mouth of the Industrial Canal to the Orleans Parish line at the Rigolets. Moving eastward from Seabrook, there was/is the New Orleans Lakefront Airport, Southshore Harbor Marina, Bally's Casino boat, hundreds of camps with Lincoln Beach amid them and numerous restaurants across Hayne Boulevard, Little Woods camps to the east of Paris Road and more camps and restaurants scattered along Irish Bayou and Chef Menteur Highway.

Lawrence Roger claimed to have purchased much of the Little Woods area from the U.S. government and settled in 1872 before the railroad came through fifteen years later. He built and rented camps but also sold some of the property. He reserved the marsh as a duck farm, where he hosted hunters.

In 1998, Hurricane Georges spared the city but did tremendous damage on the lakefront. The storm's thirty hours of fifty-mile-per-hour winds, pounding surf and tidal surge destroyed more than 80 of the approximately 110 camps along the seven-mile stretch between the Bally's casino and the eastern edge of Little Woods. Gone was the seventy-five-year-old Alma's Cottage near Paris Road and so many others of historic importance. In 1999, the Historic District Landmarks Commission nominated the camps area as a protected district. Hurricane Katrina (2005) wiped away all but one of them.

BARBOT & ALLEN

On Sunday, May 29, 1887, the New Orleans and Northeastern Railroad (also known as the Queen and Crescent Route) began Sunday and daily excursions to a "Delightful Resort on Lake Pontchartrain" that offered "Music, Dancing, Fishing, Bathing" and "Splendid Dinner with wine, 75¢" or "Fine Lunch with wine, 40¢." So said Barbot & Allen, the posters of the advertisement.

On June 18, 1887, a *Daily Picayune* article (obviously an advertisement in semi-disguise) described Little Woods as "one of the most delightful resorts in the vicinity of New Orleans…14 miles from the city." The twenty-minute train ride led to "shady groves, fine bathing, excellent fishing." Barbot & Allen had a five-year lease and built a house with a restaurant and dining room, as well as apartments for private parties. It also boasted of a well-stocked saloon, covered dancing platform for fifty couples, an excellent band, a fleet of sailboats and skiffs, as well as special excursions from the Cotton Press Depot.

But the greatest enticement may have been the bathhouses on wheels. The article elaborates: "Small white shells fringe the border [of the lake],

A circa 1908 view, not of Lake Pontchartrain, but of bathing machines, which were once on its shore. *George Eastman House Photography Collection.*

and over these the bathhouses are rolled into the depth of water required. The bather steps out on a bottom free of shells and stones." Also known as "bathing machines," these were drawn into and out of the water by a migrating horse that was moved from one "machine" to another as needed. Ladies entered on the shore fully clothed, changed into their bathing regalia and emerged for a swim.

The proprietors also provided for "picnic and excursion parties of ladies, with or without escorts…guaranteeing the fullest freedom from outside intrusion, as Little Woods is within the city limits, has a secure jail and stalwart officers always on duty."

By July, William A. Barbot was arrested for writing a Whitney National Bank check for the $12.50 he had spent on lumber to build the dancing platform, but the firm of Barbot & Allen had no account there. He also tried to pass a $10.00 check from the Bank of Commerce, where he had no funds. To make matters worse, come December, Barbot, Allen and another partner were being sued for failing to pay for two carloads of lumber, quite possibly used to build the house described earlier as well as those rolling bathhouses. Barbot & Allen never advertised its grand resort in Little Woods again.

1890s

Shooting matches and target practice were popular amusements in Little Woods in the 1890s. The Washington Artillery was there for contests in 1893 and 1895. The Queen and Crescent/Northeastern Sunday Excursion Trains were available for picnickers.

A *Times-Picayune* 1895 report speaks of Little Woods as an island in winter and, except for the railroad, reachable only by boat during high waters. But in summertime, it was a breezy resort comprising old oak trees and a sandy shell beach with excellent bathing and fishing facilitates. And new camps were sprouting up.

The Not in the Trust Rod and Gun Club, whose president, steamboat captain T.P. Leathers, was an advocate and excellent competitor, spent much time here shooting and then, of course, dining. In 1897, the Louisiana State Rifle League held a grand outing with matches and other amusements. That same year, the Crescent Rod and Gun Club opened new headquarters with an elaborate dinner.

In 1892, the Little Woods Resort and bathhouse was up for auction, and in 1896, the eleven-passenger steamer *Cupid*, owned by its captain, John L. Trasher, was scheduled to run in Little Woods. More camps, restaurants and improvements made Little Woods more attractive as a resort. Politician and sportsman Charles H. Morel's Gray Gables cottage was quite popular. Catching one hundred fish in a short period of time was not an unusual phenomenon, lending credence to Little Woods's reputation as prime fishing grounds.

An example of the fun to be had in 1917 was a truck ride to Peter Winkler's Margaret camp/restaurant / dance hall, with Mendoza's Ragtime Band providing the music for dancing. The day could be spent fishing and boating. In 1922, it was raided for serving liquor and was shut down temporarily in 1930 for violating liquor laws.

THE RUBIE

In 1915, Helen Bourda's grandparents opened the Rubie off Hayne Boulevard. By 1921, the Rubie offered dinners and jazz bands, and it rented "sanitary camps at moderate prices." In 1923, Helen was born there, and she would become one of the best-known residents of Little Woods until its final days. The family once had fifteen camps, "and we never had no electricity or running water till I was 18 years old," Helen said.

In the year she was born, a *Times-Picayune* advertisement gives a good description of what the Rubie was and what it had to offer. The Rubie "Made Little Woods Famous" with its bathing and picnic crowds, dinner for $1.00 and "gumbo, turtle soup, soft shell crabs, spring chicken, stuffed crabs, sandwiches, all kinds of salads," as well as "dancing every night—all day Sunday." It was simply the "most popular place in Little Woods"—all that for an admittance of "weekdays 25¢/adults 15¢/children, Sundays 50¢ and 15¢." Plenty of parking space was on the Rubie's grounds, and other camps were also available for rent.

Another 1923 ad seeks a "GOOD piano player. night work. $25 week. board and lodging. Phone Long Distance," which tells us how serious the Rubie was about the music played there and just how remote Little Woods was back in the day.

Louis Rudolf Moreau Sr. died in 1945 at age fifty-three. He was a native of Milneburg, the father of Louis Jr., Charles F. and Alan E. His family

A group picnic and the Rubie in the 1920s. *Louisiana Digital Library.*

Hayne Boulevard in 1938. *Louisiana Digital Library.*

operated restaurants in Milneburg and Little Woods for three generations, the last in Little Woods, which was the Rubie.

In the late 1940s, the Rubie provided picnic tables and swimming, crabbing and fishing facilities for a mere twenty-five cents on weekdays and fifty cents on Sundays. In the early 1950s, Helen and her mother were taking reservations for the Rubie's facilities, which included a one-hundred-by-one-hundred-foot dance hall, a jukebox, a shelter and picnic tables for the same price. In 1951, Charles Moreau (Helen's husband and Louis's son) was operating the business.

In 1953, Joseph "Papa" Bourda sold the Ruby (advertised for sale with this alternate spelling as a 93-by-135-foot lot, restaurant, bar and "pleasure resort"). He then opened Bourda's restaurant and bar at the end of Hayne Boulevard at Paris Road. That same year, a "New Ruby's Restaurant" opened (but never acquired the reputation of the original), and the levee board's threat to demolish camps to fill the area for recreation and the proposed enlargement of the Lakefront Airport did not come to pass.

Helen Bourda, born at the Rubie, holds a painting of her family home and birthplace in 1988. Times-Picayune.

Bourda's Restaurant and (mostly) bar still remains in its old spot at the end of Hayne. Helen ran it for years. It was a one-stop shop for those wanting to know the most minute detail of Little Woods news or gossip. It was where old-timers hung out to share stories of the past and present. Bourda's also hosted private picnics on the large, tree-laden property in the rear, dances, parties and shrimp and crab boils. Bourda's Pavilion across the road on the lake did the same until Hurricane Georges washed it away in 1998.

One of the most famous camps on the lake, the Rubie, was taken down by Hurricane Hilda in 1964. A note of interest: Helen Bourda's aunt (her mother's sister) was Rubie Rodriguez Taylor. One cannot help but wonder if the Rubie was named after her.

Lake Shore Drive Tavern

In 1919, Northern States Realty acquired a huge portion of land largely drained by its previous owner, the Lake Shore Land Company, which had named the entire area Pontchartrain Groves. Northern States began touting the the old road along the shore as Lake Shore Drive and predicted that the company would make it comparable to the same-named grand boulevard along Lake Michigan.

The company also planned a twenty-room hotel and one-hundred-seat restaurant with a three-hundred-foot pier, bathhouses and dressing rooms. In May 1921, company president Frank B. Todd held the first dinner at the Lake Shore Drive Tavern for local luminaries, including Frank B. Hayne, who had been a leading figure in the Lake Shore Land Company. Fred Ernest was facilities manager, serving fish and chicken dinners to folks who danced to the Blue Ribbon Jazzers. Ernest also operated the five-hundred-foot bathing pier.

The 1921 Mayer Israel employee picnic was held there; workers met at the Canal Street store accompanied by a band. On their arrival at the lake, there was dancing, boating, bathing, games, contests and dinner.

By 1923, Northern States had, after calling the area "Citrus," renamed it "Edgewater," and the hotel had been built but put up for lease. Apparently, the Lake Shore Drive moniker failed to stick—a classified ad offered "Little Woods Road Hotel and Café…20 rooms, tub and shower baths. Cafe-2 dining rooms, 30x40. Dance floors, screened galleries…landscaped grounds. Bathing, boating, fishing." It is possible that this place later became the Happy Landing (see later in the chapter).

Luthjens

The coming of the seawall and the lakefront airport resulted in the end of camps and businesses at Seabrook, the area at the mouth of the Industrial Canal. But before predictions of that threat, in 1922, the New Seabrook Bathhouse, built by John W. Luthjens, opened 1,280 feet from the mouth of the canal. In 1925, Luthjens was elected president of the Bathhouse Operators Association, which consisted of thirty owners organized to protest the more immediate problem: pollution laws that threatened their closings. The group also purportedly sought to improve the sanitary conditions of its businesses. It survived long enough that, in 1927, Luthjens's bathhouse and restaurant were raided to uncover twenty-four cases of homebrew beer, seventy-five bottles of beer on ice and beer manufacturing equipment.

Paris Royal Roof Garden

William H. Paris was the proprietor of his self-named Paris Royal Roof Garden on Little Woods Road at Seabrook. It was a two-story camp with a restaurant serving filet mignon and fresh seafood. There was also a long bathhouse consisting of two rows of lockers equipped with showers to accommodate hundreds of swimmers. Popular for music and dancing, it may have been even more well known as a gambling venue. The May 31, 1926 edition of the *Times-Picayune* reported, "Dance Goes On as Police Raid Seabrook Place"—thirteen people were arrested while the house band, Deichman's Moonlight Serenaders, was instructed by the raiders to play louder so as not to attract attention to their intention. An estimated one hundred patrons swam and danced, either unaware or disinterested in the police activity. Charges were filed, and two police wagons were needed to confiscate the gambling equipment.

Carlson's

Seaman Oscar Albert Carlson, a native of Oskarshamm, Sweden, settled in New Orleans in 1900. He owned and operated Carlson's Grocery, restaurant, bar and dance hall east of Parish Road in Little Woods. He was also the first school bus driver in the area, transporting students in Little Woods, Citrus and Edgewater some fifteen miles to and from Gentilly Terrace Elementary in his vehicle emblazoned with "Oscar Carlson, Little Woods, LA." A photo of it, from 1921, appeared in the August 2, 1990 *Times-Picayune*.

Carlson's featured early jazz bands, including the Camelia Jazz Band in 1922. Active in his community, in 1936, Oscar Carlson was vice-president of the Little Woods Lakeshore Property Owners and Residents Improvement Association. His bar and grocery, with its jukebox, wide front walk and benches out front lasted until midcentury. Oscar died in 1955.

1920s–1930s

In 1927, proprietors/brothers Henry and Nicholas Herzog opened the New Modern Midway restaurant and bathhouse (with five hundred bathing suits for rent) at Seabrook. Albert Brunies and His Orchestra, the house band, performed on its roof garden.

Leon Loverde's camp between the Margaret and the Rubie was up for auction in 1929, as was the Pleasure camp and bathhouse. A good description of Loverde's as an example of other such places appeared in a classified for-sale ad: "dance hall, lockers, three bed rooms, porches all around, galvanized roof, kitchen separate from house, power houses, large bath house with 12 bath houses and two bedrooms in rear."

In 1930, levee board president Abe Shushan opined that removal of the camps was necessary "to facilitate progress" for the airport, which would not open until 1934. This was but one of many threats through the years. The approximately 230 camps between the Industrial Canal and Little Woods remained for many years after. But Peter Winkler's Margaret camp, Charles Holand and Henry J. Hillerbrand's Palace and Louis Moreau's Restaurant and Bathhouse did not fare as well. They were shut down (perhaps temporarily) in 1930 for violating liquor laws. That same year, the Lakeside Inn was operated by Mrs. L. Harman at Seabrook. In the 1930s, Big Ben's

March 19, 1930 front-page news announcing the unanimous vote by the Orleans Levee Board to remove all shoreline camps from the Industrial Canal to Little Woods. Times-Picayune.

Cottage and Romer's Camp hosted parties, and Ebler's Camp was planning to open.

The state health department ordered all private camps from Bucktown to Little Woods (four hundred of which existed east of Industrial Canal) to be closed in 1931 because of pollution from dumped sewage bacteria. None of them was shut down.

MAMA LOU'S

Exactly when Mama Lou's first opened, and the identity of its namesake, are mysteries (to this writer), but Mama Lou is said to have been a jazz musician who appeared to be eighty or so years old in the mid-1950s. Located on Hayne Boulevard near what is now Crowder Road, this camp was famous for its entertainment—bands, dancing and seafood.

The earliest known musician to have performed at Mama Lou's was blues guitarist and composer Richard "Rabbit" Brown, who died around 1937 after having regularly played there.

Jazz cornetist Eddie Dawson began playing regularly there with Andrew Jefferson and Andrew Morgan's Band in 1939. Herb Morand's Jazz Band was a regular during the 1940s. Trumpeter Louis "Kid Shots" Madison performed in the mid-1940s. In 1946, fourteen-year-old trumpeter Frank Assunto, his seventeen-year-old brother and trombonist Fred and other

Raymond Glapion on the guitar and Eddie Dawson on the bass are captured here playing at Mama Lou's in 1950. "Jitterbugging Not Allowed" reads the sign (*upper right*). *Louisiana Digital Collection.*

A 1961 view of Mama Lou's, when it was owned by Frank and Rita Lipps. *Louisiana Digital Collection.*

teenagers (including very young clarinetist Pete Fountain) began playing on Saturdays at Mama Lou's. Peter Bocage, with Eddie Dawson, had regular gigs here from 1949 through 1954.

In the early 1950s, Charlie Jaeger bought the business. In 1960, the gay Krewe of Yuga held its third annual ball, with Pete Fountain and the Assunto brothers performing. Mama Lou's remained a public venue until at least 1961, when it was purchased by Frank and Rita Lipps. Hurricane Betsy damaged it and many other camps in the area in 1965.

Happy Landing

The Happy Landing dinner and dancing club, established by local stage actor Ferdinand Paul Lafon Sr., opened at 6408 Hayne Boulevard in 1932. Named for its proximity to the proposed Shushan/Lakefront Airport, which opened two years later, it was improved in 1938 with renovations and a new stucco Mediterranean-style façade and a bright neon sign that featured a fish, an airplane and a frog. (Fried frog legs was a popular delicacy.)

On the large dance floor, a nine-piece orchestra performed on Saturdays. Big band and jazz were played here by the Albert Jiles Band, with Eddie

A 1950 Happy Landing postcard. *Artist's collection.*

Dawson, Lionel Ferbos and many others. From 1947 through the 1950s, pianist and singer "Sweet" Emma Barrett was a regular. In 1954, clarinetist Israel Gorman recorded an album here that included "Eh La Bas."

The upper floor of the two-story structure was surrounded by windows to catch cool lake breezes. There was a forty-foot bar and five hundred seats—plenty of space for banquets, parties, luncheons and family dinners of seafood, steaks, turtle soup, gumbo, frog legs and much more.

A December 29, 1961 fire gutted the building, resulting in approximately $20,000 in damages. Lafon's widow, Alice Gayaut, sold the large property in 1973. The Pontchartrain Lodge Nursing Home replaced the Happy Landing (later to become the Lutheran Home for the Aged).

Wacky Ducky / Buster Brice

In 1949, George Floyd "Buster" Brice owned the cinderblock building across from Lincoln Beach at 13812 Hayne (on a 43-by-118-square-foot lot) called the Wacky Ducky. In 1957, it became known as Buster Brice's but was

Pictured here in 1957, Buster Brice's served Regal Beer and seafood and offered picnic grounds in the rear. *Historic New Orleans Collection.*

reincarnated as the Ritz Cafe early in the 1960s, when Henrietta Brice took over. In 1964, Dolores Johnson had the place, which she renamed the Wacky Ducky. The property is now occupied by New Home Family Worship Center.

EDDIE'S EDGELAKE

Edward Louis Crochet Sr. owned and operated a restaurant in Carrollton before he bought property near the airport, which, in the 1920s, developers were marketing as "Edgelake." He used the ground floor of his home at 7126 Hayne Boulevard as Eddie's Edgelake bar and restaurant. Eddie passed away in 1969, shortly after he retired, and Leo Albert Sider Sr. acquired the business. When he died in 1972, his son Leo Jr. took over. The Edgelake had a brief renaissance, so to speak, when poetry readings as well as jazz, 'blues and brass combos performed there in 2005. As of this writing, the old building sits abandoned and neglected.

A 1953 view of the camps, from Hayne Boulevard. *Louisiana Digital Library.*

Deanie's

In 1957, Jay's Bar, Restaurant, and Grocery was operated by L.J. Joubert at 7350 Hayne. In 1972, the three-thousand-square-foot improved property was operated by Charles Smith and Joseph Lopinto. It became Lopinto's Restaurant and Bar in 1973, when it was purchased by Joseph P. Lopinto Sr. By 1977, Charles Joseph Bourgeois was running Lopinto's.

Dolores "Deanie" Accardo had a cafeteria in town at 3930 Euphrosine Street (later Sucre Confection Studio) before opening her popular seafood restaurant here in 1979. She gave credit to the neighboring Lakeview Seafood for inventing the seafood boat but also recognized that "spillover" from those not wishing to wait in long lines there helped her gain loyal customers. Katrina came and went, but Deanie's reopened as quickly as possible. In 2011, Deanie transferred ownership to her daughter Phylis Accardo but was still working on Hayne in 2016 at age eighty-two.

Bright Light

The road was still muddy and potholed when Bright Light bar and restaurant opened at 10800 Hayne around 1960—its light served as a beacon for those seeking seafood dinners or a cold draft or two. In 1978, it became the Tip Top Lounge and Restaurant owned by Frank Inge and Mark Frandsen, who did all the all cooking and catering. But by 1990, it was known as Henry's House restaurant and bar, as it is today.

Gee and Lil's

Lillian and Virgil George "Gee" Crochet cooked at his father, Eddie's, Edgelake restaurant for fourteen years before opening Gee and Lil's at 7204 Hayne in 1962 on the opposite corner of Hayne. (Their house was behind the restaurant.) They served seafood, fried chicken, steaks and other typical neighborhood-style fare. Atypical was the stuffed two-headed calf mounted and hung behind the bar above the terrazzo floor—it had been born at a nearby dairy at Read and Morrison Roads.

Gee and Lil's was a family affair. Lil's brother designed the building, which had two private banquet rooms, and her sisters, nieces and nephews worked there. Gee's brother Eddie often tended bar. Few batted an eye when, in 1964, Virgil was arrested for gambling and for allowing gambling at his bar and restaurant—nothing unusual about that.

Gee died in 1975, when he was only fifty years old, but Lil held on to the place with the same old jukebox, fifty-cent draft beers and one-dollar mixed drinks and kept cooking here until 1986, when she sold it. In 1987, still under the Gee and Lil's name, John-Christopher Ward with native Jamaican chef Cecil Palmer began serving spicy Jamaican/Caribbean and Creole cooking. In 1990, Larry G. Willis bought the restaurant, still named for the original owners. Russell Kelly and his wife, Lynn, opened Jayde's Jazzy Soul Food Joint around 1995, closing in 1997 to become Dorothy's in 2002. In 2003, Malcolm Gibson gained tentative approval to a zoning change that would allow him to open an embalming facility on the property. Neighbors objected. That fate never came to the old Gee and Lil's site. The restaurant has been demolished, along with its wonderful neon signs.

Lakeview Seafood

Lakeview Seafood and Steak House was opened at 7400 Hayne some time before 1964 by Richard C. Weixel and Maurice R. Blondeau. In 1965, it was listed as belonging to D.C. Howze and, in 1968, by Mae Downey. This unpretentious restaurant gained fame when Charles Marcus Smith and his wife, Evelyn, took over around 1969 and then introduced the "original Oyster Boats and Shrimp Boats." Like many seafood houses of the time, their seafood platter contained shrimp, oysters, catfish, trout, stuffed (in the shell) crabs, fried softshell crab and frog legs, all included in the price, even into the 1980s. Mr. Smith died in 1981 at age fifty-three, but his family continued the business. Daughter Beth Hollaway stepped up as chef, and by 1986, daughters Reenie Smith and Laura Jennewine were working there. In 1987, the boats were still a bargain at $15.50 for the combo or $14.50 for the single seafood (fish, oysters or shrimp), which easily fed two or more. But even waiting in the long line that wound along the side of the restaurant at its peak of popularity offered no "view" of the lake, only of the levee. The food was worth the wait.

Lincoln Beach sits amid scores of camps in this Leon Trice photo, circa 1950. *New Orleans Public Library.*

Across Hayne Boulevard, new houses were built by 1982, but the old camps remained the same. Times-Picayune.

Only five of about seventy camps along Hayne survived Hurricane Georges in 1998. Little Woods was luckier; the storm claimed five of about twenty-five camps east of Paris Road. Times-Picayune.

After Hurricane Katrina blasted through the city, only one camp remained, the same one that had survived Georges. Times-Picayune.

Robert and Rita Bourgeois took over in 1988 as Rita's Lakeview Seafood with new floors, additional windows, improved air conditioning and seats for ninety-six diners. They introduced the "Pirogue" and had plans for expansion. The restaurant was still there in 1993 but then faded into history. The building no longer stands.

In earlier days, this place had been Jenkx and Saba's Bar and Seafood and Grocery Store (before 1958), owned by Collie K. Saba and Mrs. Joseph H. Jenks, then it became simply Jenks Bar, then Joe's Bar, run by Leon J. Delorette (1959), Old Original with Alex McInerney (1963) and Urban Toro's Toro's Place (1964).

IRISH BAYOU

Steamboats began plying the twelve miles from New Orleans to Irish Bayou for fishermen excursions beginning in the 1800s, but no on-land building sites existed until a three-fourth-mile strip of earth was created by dredging mud and sand from the lake on which to build U.S. Highway 11. The community's first permanent settler is said to have been Tony Rodriguez, who had a houseboat on the bayou in the 1930s when he planned a business renting fishing skiffs. During the 1930s and '40s, more camps for commercial fishers and crabbers began to appear and then restaurants for city people to visit.

THE BUNGALOW

During the 1930s, Pete Saperaan opened his Bungalow Camp as a fishing spot for has patrons. By the mid-1940s, it was taken over by Gene Richmond and Scott Reinecke, who hosted fishing rodeos, sold bait and served food and drinks. During the 1949 Pan-American Boat Show at the Municipal Auditorium, the Bungalow introduced the Aquacycle, a noiseless, motorless boat-propulsion device with an aluminum seat and backrest and a bicycle-style foot pedal for hands-free fishing on the run (a fisherman-propelled trolling "motor").

By the 1950s, the Bungalow was a one-stop shop/resort. Remodeled and enlarged, it included a boat launch, dock, icehouse, bait and tackle shop with

A 1952 advertisement for the new and improved Bungalow at Irish Bayou. Times-Picayune.

boats and motors for rent and a filling station that serviced boats and cars and offered road service. One could buy package liquor, cigarettes and such or dine at the restaurant, drink at the bar or party in the banquet rooms. As an example of the quality of fishing by the Bungalow, on September 28, 1945, three commercial fishers hand-lining caught three hampers of "Bull" croakers weighing a total of 650 pounds in three hours.

In 1952, Mr. and Mrs. L.E. (Gene) Richmond bought Reinecke's share and began hosting dances and floor shows on Saturdays and Sundays. In the mid-1950s, they offered box lunches to go for fishers, hot boiled crabs and crab parties, as well as fresh- and saltwater fishing supplies and facilities. But in 1958, Gene put the entire enterprise up for sale—five hundred waterfront feet of property that now included air-conditioned tourist cabins.

1950s–Katrina (2005)

In 1959, Jeff Wickes opened Bayou View restaurant and boat dock. It burned down in 1967. By the late 1960s, the old-timers were dying out or selling to "city people." In 1969, there were seventy-five permanent residences and many vacation homes/camps.

In 1986, the population hovered around seven hundred, but many of the restaurants were gone and many camps were abandoned and dilapidated. The road often flooded, which contributed to the demise of the area. Still within the city limits, before Hurricane Katrina, the community comprised about one hundred homes/camps. Simon Villemarette's castle still stands, but lost in the storm was another landmark: C.T. and Christine Sims's pyramid house, which started out as "normal" until the creative couple added a pointed roof for a second story then enclosed the sides to complete the design. Some commercial fishers, crabbers, shrimpers and duck hunters still ply these marshy waters with a wonderful view of Lake Pontchartrain.

Fishing

The oldest hunting and fishing club in the United States is the Tally Ho Club on Bayou Sauvage near Chef Pass. The original dining room, built in 1815, has been incorporated into the current clubhouse. In the late 1880s, the facility was modernized with an acetylene generator for gas lighting, which replaced oil lamps. In 1905 came an electric generator, and to this day, members come to hunt waterfowl and fish and enjoy life.

During the 1960s, some thirty marinas sold bait, rented boats and lockers and provided refreshments. By 1979, there were only seven. Pollution from sewage and drainage canals, sediment kicked up by shell dredging and the replacement of natural shorelines with seawalls and rip-rap resulted in a declining lake. But some marina owners contended that in the 1970s, insurance for their businesses was either impossible to find or cost prohibitive. By 1979, only the following establishments existed. The forty-six-year-old Gilbert's Marina was opened in 1933 by Gilbert Cousins at the north end of the Highway 11 bridge. In the 1950s, he had thirty boats for rent, but by 1979, he averaged fewer than eight per weekend. The forty-one-year-old Fishermen's Reef was opened in 1938 by Claire Bourgeois. There was also the thirty-two-year-old (George and Agnes) McEwen's Bathhouse and

Marina on Salt Bayou, which opened in 1947. The thirty-year-old (Ed) Lombard's Marina and Bait Center on the Chef Highway opened in 1949. Fred Knect's twenty-seven-year-old Rigolets Marina by Fort Pike opened in 1952. Jimmy Bateman's Bayou View Marina on Irish Bayou opened in 1967. And, finally, there was Lawrence Schaeffer's Mike's Marina on the Chef, which opened in 1974.

Benny Larmann's, at Irish Bayou for thirty-eight years since 1941, was closed by 1979, and Marques Brothers had recently sold their marina after fifty-three years (since 1926) at the Chef Bridge but kept their well-known restaurant open for a while after. In 1993, there were only two marinas on the lake renting skiffs and motors: Gilbert Cousins and his neighbor Tite's Place, both at North Shore. They are also now gone.

4

SEGREGATION ON THE SOUTH SHORE

We have been given three different bathing places upon three different occasions at the lakefront and each time were told to move on. Last year we were at Seabrook but that, too, has been taken away from us. We are not allowed in the parks, although provisions are made for ducks and geese. It is hard for us as ministers to teach our children Christianity under such circumstances…although there are 180,000 Negroes in the city and 26,000 Negro children, no facilities are available on the lakefront for Negro bathing.
—*Dr. R.W. Coleman, pastor of the First African Baptist Church, June 4, 1940,* New Orleans Times-Picayune

In Henry Righter's *Standard History of New Orleans* (1900), he notes that "the Spanish Fort has been given over to the negroes, and is a favorite place for negro picnics," or perhaps more politely, "in recent years it has become the chief resort for the colored portion of the inhabitants." Echoing the same sentiments three years later, on July 13, 1903, the *Daily Picayune* reported, "The Fort Once a Popular Resort, But Was Relegated to the Negroes…for years trains have been crowded with them.…For more than a dozen years it has been given up to negro picnics" and "fallen out of site of good society."

People of color continued to use Spanish Fort until the 1920s, when shoreline was replaced by a bulkhead and then a stepped seawall. When the original "whites only" segregated Pontchartrain Beach amusement park at the Spanish Fort shore opened in 1928, black citizens moved farther east on to Milneburg, whose town proper had been annihilated by the land reclamation.

Stepping back a century before, at its inception in 1831, the Pontchartrain Railroad planned a "colored bathhouse" in Milneburg to be located on the western side of the train wharf with a separate pier leading from the shore. When completed at a cost of $3,000 in 1833, it shared the Washington Hotel's wharf. To curtail costs, the segregated pier was scrapped. The railroad established separate cars for free people of color. Slaves could ride the train if they carried credentials or were accompanied by their owners. Upon arrival, black patrons were provided with segregated dining facilities. Until Jim Crow segregation laws were enforced in the early 1900s, blacks enjoyed the sights and sounds of Milneburg and, in fact, contributed to them as musicians.

When the second segregated Pontchartrain Beach opened at Milneburg in 1939, black New Orleanians migrated even farther east to enjoy the lake—down to Seabrook, which had been a popular shore for swimming, now at the end of the new seawall at the mouth of the Industrial Canal.

Seabrook

The land reclamation project reached the Seabrook area by 1927. In February 1928, a second batch of fill created a "beach" eight feet higher than the lake surface. In July, the Orleans Levee Board granted temporary permission for a blacks-only swimming area between Peoples Avenue and the Industrial Canal (now the area containing the UNO Lakefront Arena/Maestri Field ballpark), but only after a request by "a prominent Negro organization."

Dilkerstorn Amusement Company and Henry Eastin were each granted permits good until November 1, 1928, to operate bathhouses on the condition that they pay for lifeguards and police under the supervision of the board. Blacks swimming outside the designated area would be arrested. If any laws were broken there, the permits would be revoked.

The swimming area was reportedly large enough to accommodate six thousand persons a day. By August, thousands of swimmers enjoyed the "beach," but few were patronizing the bathhouse or concessions. The Dilkerstorn company reported that it was not reaping enough profit to pay the lifeguards and police, and it asked the levee board to do so. The board

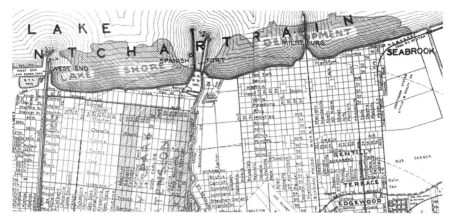

The Seabrook area (*upper right*), east of Milneburg, as it appeared in 1924. *Louisiana Digital Library.*

refused and shut down the beach. But within days, the board reversed the decision with plans to reopen the area until November, when additional filling was scheduled for the reclamation project.

An estimated one hundred white residents and real estate developers, including the New Orleans Real Estate Board, appeared before the levee board in February 1929 to protest Seabrook opening for the summer. They stated that they feared their property values would decline if a black swimming area was designated near their homes and businesses. The board responded that the beach would be closed due to more reclaimed sand being pumped in the area and assured the protesters that no temporary or permanent black swimming area had been designated and that their assistance would be asked before finalization of any plan. In March of that year, the New Orleans Real Estate Board listed opposition to a black bathing beach on the lakefront as one of its major accomplishments.

In 1930, with prompting from a delegation led by Walter Cohen (a well-respected black community leader), Abe Shushan (president of the levee board) assured the group that a black beach would be located along the seawall but could not say where. As reported in the October 21, 1931 edition of the *Times-Picayune*, property owners from four nearby subdivisions—Gentilly Terrace, Gentilly Gardens, Edgewood and the Franklin Avenue area—presented a petition signed by 2,600 residents in protest of improvements for a black American beach. Spokesperson Arthur M. Schneider warned that if the project went forward, "there are many people in the Gentilly area who would take the law into their own hands." Shushan responded that the location of a black bathing area had yet to be finalized. The citizen group had met previously to discuss the issue, and some proffered that the best location would be between the London Avenue Canal and Spanish Fort (an early version of "Not in My Back Yard").

Editors of the *Times-Picayune* wrote, in the October 22, 1931 issue, that years of postponement in selecting a permanent beach location had resulted in "protests, grievances, and bitterness....This newspaper does not advocate any particular site, it does share however the general community belief that in fairness and justice the city's Negro population should be allotted a bathing beach for its own use." Shortly thereafter, a lifeguard was provided at Seabrook.

By 1932, black New Orleanians were still swimming at Seabrook, when not being chased away. Meanwhile, the Gentilly Terrace Association was forming a committee to prevent their use of the beach. In June 1933, the Orleans Levee Board granted E.J. Lamothe a permit to operate a store and concession for Negro bathers on the shore at Seabrook.

The *Times-Picayune* spoke out again on September 22, 1935: "Some provisions should be made for a Negro beach" at Lake Pontchartrain, adding that blacks "have been permitted to use its waters, provided they did not get in the way of white bathers, in which case they were moved somewhere else. Recently down shore," where the conditions were unsafe for swimming. This likely refers to what would become Lincoln Beach on Hayne Boulevard, where, the *Picayune* noted, there was one refreshment building and a dressing room much too small to accommodate the number of bathers.

The caption of this 1930s WPA photograph of Seabrook reads "Negro section of the seawall." *Louisiana Digital Library.*

In 1937, the levee board announced that, at the request of the concessionaire, the Seabrook site would be relocated to a permanent location three-fourths of a mile from Shushan Airport with a $168,000 outlay. In 1938, the levee board changed the plan, this time announcing that a new black beach would be built about seven miles down Hayne Boulevard. It would include a tunnel under the railroad tracks, ten acres of land and seventeen thousand trees—all to be ready before the end of the year (it wasn't). Bids were put out for fill at Pontchartrain Beach and the new black beach, but it wasn't until several years later that anyone was allowed to swim there.

The 1938 City Guide informed visitors that swimming was allowed all along the Lakeshore drive seawall between West End and Little Woods, but for blacks, only one place was allowed, just west of the Shushan Airport, where the seawall ends (Seabrook).

In September 1939, black citizens asked to again be permitted to swim at Seabrook. The answer was no, and they were told that their new site would open the following year (it did

Miss Helen Fernandez, first Seabrook Bathing Beauty Contest winner, sponsored by the St. John Berchman's Insurance Company in 1938. *Creolegen.com.*

not). The Black League for the Preservation of Constitutional Rights and other groups protested. Meanwhile, the all-white Pontchartrain Beach opened with much fanfare.

During the summer of 1947, the city provided free swimming lessons at nine sites for white children and one for blacks—at Seabrook. In 1968 and '69, the Orleans Levee Board provided four lifeguards at Seabrook and opened bidding for a new sand beach there and a well to pump fresh underground water into the lake in an effort to dilute pollution (with no guarantee of success). A New Orleans Police Department program to bus underserved children to Seabrook had been suspended due to this pollution. During the 1970s, lifeguards were provided at Seabrook, but in the mid- to late 1980s, Seabrook was closed again due to pollution (apparently that water well didn't do the trick). The old "Negro Beach," when not shut down, continued to be used, and as of this writing, it still is.

LINCOLN BEACH

In 1940, the WPA provided additional funding and workers for the new black beach. The levee board declared, in February of that year, that the project was 80 percent completed but work was suspended awaiting a needed $20,000 more from the WPA. By April, a $38,000 application went to the WPA and a reported one hundred men were working on the new beach. Bids went out in May for a bathhouse and groundskeeper; at the July levee board meeting, A.G. Rickerfor bid $9,000 and had the $1,500 certified check required as a deposit. Thomas Arculeer bid $18,000 but failed to produce a deposit check, because, he said, he had been traveling to take care of amusement park business elsewhere, had just arrived back home and didn't have time to secure a certified check. After deliberation, the board deadlocked on who should win the bid. This required that the bidding remain open until the next meeting. By December, the bidding was still up for grabs, but Arculeer, in the end, secured the contract. Meanwhile, blacks were swimming at Seabrook, this time under the protection of a lifeguard, but only after their ministers united to demand free space in City Park and at Seabrook.

On April 8, 2017, the New Water Music concert produced by New Orleans Airlift featured the Louisiana Philharmonic Orchestra accompanied by one hundred musicians in boats and onshore at Seabrook. New Orleans Advocate.

In January 1941, the Orleans Levee Board, which had "planned" to open the new beach in the summer, was suddenly concerned with the lack of sanitation facilities in the surrounding 170 camps and threatened to revoke their permits unless they came into compliance. In February, the state board of health declared that camp septic tanks were not adequate to ensure a healthy swimming area. By March, the state had decided that if sanitation in Littlewoods was not improved, the camps would be shut down and the beach project would need to be abandoned. In April, work halted on the beach. However, in early May, the New Orleans City Health Department recommended that if the Citrus Canal pumping station were chlorinated, then 80 percent of harmful agents could be removed, but with the caveat that unless the camps connected to city sewage, it would not be wise for the black beach to open, and that, in fact, it would not approve its opening otherwise. By May 21, the city had reversed its decision, stating that the canal pollution only affected a one-mile radius into the lake and would not affect the beach, which was three miles away.

In this January 25, 1953 full-page ad, the levee board announced its "improvements slated for accomplishment," including work at Lincoln Beach, while proclaiming to bring "to the beautiful lakefront superior recreational facilities for all the people of New Orleans." Times-Picayune.

The long-promised permanent "Negro Beach" was unofficially opened to swimmers in the summer of 1941, but legal wranglings in June resulted in its opening and closing over health issues. However, one of its early uses included a recreation area for "Negro soldiers" from Louisiana and Mississippi. The National Park Service oversaw Civilian Conservation Corps workers in the construction of concrete tent pads. The facility was planned to accommodate five hundred semi-permanent and five hundred more temporary stays. This "housing" consisted of tents with heaters and stovepipes. Also during World War II, African American soldiers were marched fifteen miles from Jackson Barracks to the beach for mock wargames.

With WPA funding, the levee board constructed a bathhouse, shelter, paved walks and a shell parking area—all of which were a far cry from work completed by the same agencies at the all-white Pontchartrain Beach. On June 7, 1942, the improved Lincoln Beach opened with rides, concessions, games and a bar and restaurant with a dance floor.

In January 1946, the Orleans Levee Board again sought bids for a bathhouse and also for a pavilion and a groundskeeper for the facility, which was scheduled to re-open in May of that year. In July, board president William P. Dillon stated that Lincoln Beach was out of reach of public transportation and that Negros were still swimming at Seabrook, which had no facilities. In 1949, a levee board spokesperson described the beach as being in "deplorable shape" due to hurricanes during the prior two years.

Work Starts on Lincoln Beach Entrance, Shelter

—Sketch by August Perez and Associates, Architects.

CONTRACT WAS AWARDED THIS WEEK for certain items of work at Lincoln Beach. Boh Brothers Construction Company started work on the $243,000 project. Work includes an entrance sign, two bus shelters, concrete bus turn, three pedestrain underpasses, asphalt parking area, new lighting, all concrete midways for future concessions, underground drainage, etc. The project is to be completed by April 26 of this year. Design is by August Perez and Associates, architects.

Work was contracted in 1954 for $248,000 in improvements: a sign along Hayne Boulevard, a paved parking lot, two bus shelters, additional underpasses under the railroad tracks and a concrete midway, with plans for reopening in April 1954. Times-Picayune.

Opening day, 1955. Times-Picayune.

In 1953, a half-million-dollar renovation promised the conversion of the original bathhouse into a restaurant with ground and roof terraces, a freshwater pool, a wading pool, a diving pool, a new bathhouse with three thousand lockers, shelters and an expanded and rebuilt midway—all scheduled for opening in May of that year. In July, a tribute to levee board president Louis Roussell included three orchestras on the midway, a spiritual singers competition, male and female talent contests, a jitterbug contest and diving shows. Three black radio personalities—Okie Dokie, Daddy-O and Honey Chik—presided as masters of ceremonies.

On Wednesday, June 29, 1955, a "Grand Opening" was celebrated after an additional $2 million in improvements, which included a water-purification plant, a 3,500-car parking lot, a roller coaster and other rides. A new administration building was under

Even Davy Crocket was there, soon after the 1955 grand opening. Times-Picayune.

Thousands of children learned to swim at Lincoln Beach's Pee Wee swimming program, offered from 1957 to 1963. Pictured here are students and instructor Edward X. Dunn on August 14, 1960. Times-Picayune.

Abandoned, dilapidated and graffiti-riddled, Lincoln Beach was still used by some New Orleanians years after closing. This photograph was taken in 1977. Times-Picayune.

construction, designed to include an air-conditioned, soundproof, rooftop garden; Carver House restaurant; and a cocktail lounge.

In 1957, Lincoln Beach opened its midway to the Negro State Fair, where citizens from all around Louisiana could enjoy the midway, Kiddieland, the Penny Arcade and Shooting Gallery, the Fun House and the Rock-O-Plane. The Carter House offered fine dining, banquet facilities and a casual rooftop terrace.

Through the years, Ray Charles, Sam Cooke, Little Richard, the Ink Spots, Fats Domino, Earl King, Ernie K-Doe, Irma Thomas, the Neville Brothers and Deacon John performed at Lincoln Beach.

The 1964 federal order prohibiting the operation of segregated facilities was followed by a July 6, 1964 notice from the operating Lincoln Beach Corporation giving thirty days' notice for cancellation of the lease. Lincoln Beach closed on Wednesday, August 5, 1964.

On Tuesday, October 15, 1968, the levee board sought bids for lease of the property "as is," with the requirement that it be operated as a public recreational area prohibited from operating amusement rides. There were no takers for the 1,420 feet of lakeshore land and the 700-foot parking lot. Fifty years later, hulking skeletons of abandoned buildings remained untouched. After Katrina, a T-wall and access gate were constructed at the Hayne Boulevard side of this site.

5

ST. TAMMANY

S teamboats were the initial form of travel between New Orleans and the St. Tammany resorts until the five-mile Watson-Williams Bridge from New Orleans East to what is now Eden Isles (near Slidell) opened on February 18, 1928. In 1930, the Rigolets Bridge from Fort Pike was under construction, and in 1936, the last steamer landed at Mandeville, marking the end of an era of leisurely and entertaining travel across the lake. The Causeway, from Metairie to Mandeville, opened in 1956.

HOWZE BEACH

Some day a group of Louisiana projectors are confident they will create an Eden of the St. Tammany section bordering the lake, not far from the Chef, to which they have given the name Howze Beach.
—Times-Picayune, *October 18, 1925*
(The name Howze Beach later fell out of fashion, to be replaced decades later with the designation Eden Isles.)

Longtime steamboat captain James B. Howze, a member of the St. Tammany Parish Police Jury, was a self-proclaimed advocate of "Good Roads"—so much so that in 1915 he wanted visitors and locals to enjoy the beach he owned in front of his sizable landholdings. So he built a five-mile road to it from Slidell. With visions of a resort where summer cottages sprouted up out of the lake fronting his beach, he also had plans to build a restaurant and pavilion serving ice cream and soft drinks for picnickers, fishers, boaters and swimmers. He had already driven pilings for his own cottage to nest amid several already there owned by local bigwigs U.G. Neuhauser (mercantile merchant with the motto "Every Deal a Square Deal"), W.E. Gause (police jury and school board member and a descendant of Slidell's first settlers) and Andrew Canulette (shipbuilder). Howze boasted of crowds already visiting his beach, chauffeured by automobiles (four riders at a time) from Slidell for a mere thirty-five cents per round trip, with a stop along the way to a conveniently located store selling bathing suits (both enterprises no doubt backed by Captain Howze).

To prove the majesty of his beautiful road and beach, Howze invited forty-two local movers and shakers, including Fritz Salmen (brickmaking and shipbuilding) and Gause, to a fine dinner served at Neuhauser's cottage cooked by Chef Gaston Rondeau. On the menu was redfish court bouillon, stuffed crab and baked red snapper served with wine and Budweiser beer.

Howze had actually first built the road two years prior, but he had big plans now for his self-named beach (remnants of which still exist today down under the I-10 twin spans) and road (partially still remaining now parallel to the interstate). In addition, Howze expected the public road and bridges being built over Chef Menteur Pass and the Rigolets to connect with his—then visitors from far and wide could conveniently partake of his enterprises.

In 1917, the police jury approved an outlay of $150 to improve Howze Road. In 1921, the same body accepted a request from the East Pontchartrain Ferry Company for a franchise to travel from the Chef to Slidell via Howze Beach and Road for a fee of $1 per year. Also approved was permission to dredge a canal from Howze Beach into an existing channel owned by the parish and to build a wharf there. It was not long after that the police jury allotted $350 from the road fund to dredge the canal. Before the year was over, the passenger and car ferries *Mollie Lee* (Captain Virgil "V.J." "Red" Scogin; began service from Pearlington, Mississippi) and *Winnie Davis* (named for the daughter of Confederate president Jefferson Davis and owned by Captain Jim Howze) plied between New Orleans, the Chef and Howze Beach. In those early years, Howze Beach became a popular venue for parties and picnics, and the ferries hosted onboard dance parties.

When the steamboat *St. Tammany* made its first voyage between West End to Mandeville in 1910, hundreds of townspeople were there to witness the historic event. They had decorated the three-hundred-foot landing pier with bunting and Chinese lanterns. With much decorum, the boat captain and manager were presented with flowers and banners and such. But on July 20, 1924, Captain James B. Howze (then president of St. Tammany Parish) and his partner, F.M. Comfort (then mayor of Slidell), christened a new *St. Tammany* liner—a crude oil–powered, five-hundred-passenger vessel able to cross the lake in only ninety minutes while carrying twenty-five cars, making a daily business commute possible. The boat was built for Howze & Comfort Inc. by Canulette Shipyard.

In 1925, in anticipation that the planned bridges over the Chef Pass and Rigolets would enable drivers to easily reach Howze Beach, thirty charter members gathered to plan a resort and subdivision on eight thousand acres of undeveloped marshy land they planned to drain. The group began construction on a two-story Howze Beach Club house to be built on ninety creosote pilings already driven into the lake to provide for a nine-foot elevation over the water. In October, the clubhouse was completed; developer Malcolm (M.D.) Kostmayer served as master of ceremonies at its dedication—a men's- and owners-only supper party. Present, among other influential businessmen, were F.C. Codifer, Dr. C.F Gelbke, A. Neuhauser, O.B. Brugier, A.P. Boh and J.B. Howze. The clubhouse, with porches all around, an artesian well, a lighting system and a radio plant, was said to be the first hunting and fishing club home that provided a dormitory for women.

McClane City

Nearby, J.S. McClane had big plans for his own development 2.6 miles from Howze Beach. Spanish Trail Highlands offered 572 homesites at five dollars per front foot. The enterprise was apparently not meeting McClane's grand expectations; in 1928, he changed the name "Spanish Trail Highlands" to "New Slidell." It included the subdivisions Highland Park, Beach View, Central Park, Howze Beach, Homeland Heights and Spanish Trail Highlands.

He held a 1930 contest to rename "New Slidell": "That name has been loosely applied to other properties nearby…it is desirable to [specifically] identify the J.S. McClane Standard Realty Co. developments" (that is, snob appeal and upmarketing by the company president). Allegedly, thousands

Howze Beach Road can be seen in this June 20, 1926 advertisement. Times-Picayune.

of contest entries poured through the mail, but can you believe that the winner was "McClane City"?

J.S. McClane was the self-proclaimed "Sensation of the South," taking out large advertisements in local newspapers inviting all to his speaking engagements and tent shows. He lectured on "Imagination—The Mystic Power" and the "Message of Prosperity (complete with "pungent, pithy facts") during the Great Depression.

When the throngs arrived, they were provided with free food, drinks, music and stunts in McClane City, where he provided "a talk such as this country has never so far heard anywhere—The event of the century!"

By August, he reported that two thousand visitors had purchased 131 lots. In October, he claimed that six homes were under construction and that a roofing and tile works had located there. In 1931, he told of 13 more lots

Who Is This Man McClane?

These Three Pictures Give You the Answer

J. S. McClane

"Sensation of the South"

A Dynamic Thinker

A Man of Action

Herald of a New Era of Thought and Achievement

Standard General Realty Co., Inc.

In the summer of 1930, this man twice provided free bus, taxi and limousine service over the new free public highway and bridges to his "city." This August 4, 1930 full-page advertisement explained why. Times-Picayune.

sold. In 1933, J.S. McClane was charged with fraud for selling undeveloped property under the guise of it being fitted with buildings and artesian wells. In 1934, Standard Realty Co. was in receivership. His name lived on for a time; in the 1930s and perhaps into the '50s, the McClane City Night Club hosted ladies' club parties and such. Today, few local residents have any recollection or recognition of the name McClane City.

BACK AT HOWZE BEACH, the *Winnie Davis* was still piloted by Captain Howze, who now owned the North Shore Transport & Tramway Company and was offering more lots for sale. Alfred D. Danziger purchased thirteen hundred nearby acres along the shore in 1926. By 1928, M.D. Kostmayer owned the club and had dredged fifteen miles of canals for draining seven thousand acres of marshland.

A blow to further development of the over-the-lake cottage resort at Howze Beach came in that same year, when the Louisiana Supreme Court declared the beds of lakes as state property, with no other entity having the right to construct permanent structures over them. The case involved Philip Timothy, who had built a two-story public bathhouse three hundred feet offshore near the harbor of Howze Beach Club. The court decided that he had trespassed on the public domain.

Soon afterward, in 1928, the club was for sale—350 feet on the lakefront; three buildings suitable for a restaurant, a soft drink stand or dance halls; sleeping accommodations; a machine house for lighting; fifty rooms; a 700-foot run into the lake connecting to an eighteen-room bathhouse; and two pavilions on the beach. At that time, the club proprietor was Adam Matthes. Cleveland Laniere served as the cook.

"It will be a question of only a few years before this section will be the playground of the south," said Alfred D. Danziger in 1928. He embarked upon a huge reclamation project of drainage and hydraulic filling. "6,000 acres now dry and habitable" he said.

In this July 22, 1928 *Times-Picayune* advertisement, St. Tammany Harbor is prominently illustrated surrounded by Grand Lagoon Road. To the right of it is Howze Beach Road, the Howze Beach Club and the pumping station that helped turn thousands of marshy acres into solid ground. Times-Picayune.

Howze Beach Club hosted a party in 1929 to show off improvements; into the 1930s, society parties, picnics and dances were held there. In 1930, Slidell deputy sheriff M.T. Kostmayer and others were arrested while at a dinner party for shooting ducks (which they were partaking) out of season. Then the promise of steamboats and new roads and bridges bringing excursionists to Howze Beach faded, but it was, for years, still visited by occasional picnickers. In 1956, Captain Howze died.

One new road actually did spur development in the area. In 1965, the I-10 twin spans opened, landing at Howze Beach but offering no access to it. But two years later, 1,000 additional acres of marshland were drained, and by 1970, the 2,400-acre resort-styled island community Eden Isles opened with thirty-five miles of navigable waterways (canals), a $2 million country club and a marina (the former St. Tammany Harbor) in the old Grand Lagoon.

Before drainage and development, this area was widely known for fabulous duck and poule d'eau hunting. Old-timers described the sky as black with birds at peak season. Fishers remember it as among the best fishing and spawning areas along Lake Pontchartrain.

The Roof

The Roof (Carr Drive) was a beachside malt/burger stand with a jukebox. Its open rooftop was used by bands for playing music for dancing. It also had a playground, mini-carousel, pier with a slide into the lake and lifeguards from about 1958 through the early 1960s. It was operated by Allen and Gloria Clements.

Vera's

Sometime before 1940, railroad man Jake Bauer ran a bait stand and bar out of a tin-roofed shed on the gravel road at the end of a rock jetty along Lake Pontchartrain on what is now Lakeview Drive south of Slidell. It came to be known as "Old Jake's Rat's Nest." In 1952, Vera Cyrus began cooking there. Out of an old cast-iron skillet she'd fry up fishermen's catches and more. Then she and her husband, Ralph, opened their own place next door atop pilings over the lake and expanded the menu. Trapdoors in the floor allowed for seafood plate scrapings to be deposited directly back into the lake while also serving as inlets for rising storm tides that would otherwise knock out the floorboards. But the big storms—Hurricanes Audrey (1957), Betsy (1965) and Camille (1969)—washed the wood structure into the lake. The Cyruses prevailed and rebuilt. They also patched the place back together after other unnamed storms.

In 1977, Vera retired and sold her recipes and the business to her sister-in-law Clair Mattern and Clair's sons Donnie and Steve. Clair retired in 1986, but Donnie and his wife, Dena, kept the restaurant going strong until Hurricane Katrina (2005) obliterated the entire strip of land on which their beloved family business abutted. They vowed to rebuild there, yet again, but new construction codes rendered such an undertaking impossible. They did the next best thing, reopening far inland in a strip shopping center on Highway 190 / Gause Boulevard just sixteen months after Katrina. The new restaurant, of course, could never replicate the charm or the atmosphere of the old one out over Lake Pontchartrain. The Matterns had the foresight to take with them, just before Katrina, their "mascot" (a beer-drinking statuette that was created by float builder Joe Barth), the old sign and the old photographs that now grace the new place. Vera's recipes are still served along with Dena's new creations.

MANDEVILLE

New Orleans–born French Creole Bernard Xavier de Marigny de Mandeville was born into wealth and privilege. His father had extensive real estate holdings in New Orleans. In 1829, after dividing the New Orleans plantation he had inherited into the Faubourg Marigny district, he bought 2,856 acres in St. Tammany for $11,600 that became the present town of Mandeville. In 1830 and 1831, he bought more St. Tammany land on which he, with John Davis, planned a resort on the lake. Another historical account tells us that the Marigny family acquired the St. Tammany land via a French land grant, which the U.S. Congress recognized, confirming Bernard Marigny as title holder in 1832.

After plotting the town in 1834, de Mandeville published an advertisement for the sale at auction of five thousand arpents between Bayou Castine and Lewisburg along the lake. He also chartered the steamer *Blackhawk* to transport any interested parties from Milneburg to their prospective new properties at "Quartier de Mandeville," where the originator mandated that land along the shoreline remain in the public domain in perpetuity, that all but two streets (Mandeville and Jackson, which would be one hundred feet wide) be fifty feet wide and that he would construct a wharf for steamboats and a bridge across the bayou. Within three days, he realized a profit of $69,000. Many of the first lots purchased were sold to residents of the Faubourg Marigny.

As he was doing all this, de Mandeville was also buying even more property east of the bayou. In 1829, he purchased the 1,600-arpent de la Ronde plantation as well as Antoine Bonnabel's 4,024-arpent property, which included a residence, a cornmill, livestock and slaves. He named the 5,600-acre stretch of land "Fontainebleau," after the Fontainebleau Forest near Paris. He added a sugar mill, sawmill, brick kiln and infirmary. He had a canal dug to the lake to transport the goods he produced. This land would become Fontainebleau State Park, which still holds crumbling chimneys and bricks from walls of his industrial endeavor.

Fontainebleau

The trail of ownership titles to what is now Fontainebleau State Park since Marigny's ownership begins in 1852, when Hippolyte Griffin acquired it. The property then passed on to: Jean Paul Poutz (1853), Merchants Mutual Insurance Company (1874), Thomas H. Kennedy (1875), lumberman George W. Nott (1881) and the Great Southern Lumber Company (1905), which operated (reportedly) the largest sawmill in the world. In 1935, St. Tammany civic leaders fought to protect the forest, which contained trees as old as four hundred years. They also sought to declare the land a national park. That didn't come to pass, but in 1938, Fontainebleau State Park was established.

It has been said that timber from Nott's Fontainebleau was used to build the New Orleans Custom House. Mr. and Mrs. Nott also owned a home at 2627 Lakeshore Drive, believed to be one of the oldest surviving buildings in Mandeville, now known as the Morel-Nott House.

It has also been written that John James Audubon (1785–1851) spent much time at Fontainebleau painting birds and that he often claimed to have been born there. He was born in Haiti.

1830s–1870s

In April 1834, the *Blackhawk* steamboat began steady operation across Lake Pontchartrain, connecting Fontainebleau, Mandeville and Madisonville to New Orleans, providing weekly service during the summer. In 1837, the steamer *Pontchartrain* began running from New Orleans to Mandeville, Lewisburg and Madisonville three days per week and on Sunday excursions. That same year, the U.S. Mail steamer *Mobile* cruised from Milneburg to Mandeville, Lewisburg and Madisonville. The Madisonville Lighthouse went into service in 1838. Around 1840, Pierre Davis opened the Mandeville Hotel, offering food, lodging, a bathhouse, a billiard room and stables. At the end of the decade, the Stingaree Club was opened.

Due to a very low number of malaria and yellow fever deaths on the northshore, the U.S. government ranked St. Tammany as the second-healthiest place in the nation in the 1850s. "Ozone air" was believed to relieve lung and throat ailments as well as a variety of health-related maladies.

The California House, Bachelor's Hall and Mrs. Wellington's Houseboats all offered food, wine and lodging, as did Horace Lauzainghein during this decade. An 1856 storm washed away eighteen bathhouses. During the Civil War, the northshore was hard hit by lack of supplies from New Orleans and other war-related circumstances, but when the steamer *Camelia* began running from Milneburg to Mandeville and Lewisburg in 1867, the northern towns once again became popular resorts.

By the 1870s, picnics, dances, soirees and parties of all sorts were held at private homes and clubs. During a 1878 yellow fever epidemic, those who could afford to escape to the northshore did so. By 1879, six steamers plied from New Orleans to Mandeville, Madisonville and Covington: the *New Camelia* (actually the "old" one refurbished), *Abita*, *Alice*, *Georgia Muncy*, *Heroine* and *Henry Wright*. They were capable of transporting two thousand people on a Sunday. Later to come were the *Leonora*, *Ophelia*, *Hanover* (later renamed *Mandeville*) and the *Ozone* with its onboard slot machines.

The Mandeville Yacht Club (a branch of the Great Outdoors Club of St. Tammany Parish), which had a nearby clubhouse with sleeping apartments, hosted a regatta at the Crescent Hotel as its headquarters in 1896. That same year, a New Orleans Horticulturists outing included a trip across the lake on the steamer *Cape Charles*, a jaunt in Jackson Park, a side trip to Lewisburg and a function at the Crescent.

An excursion from New Orleans in 1879 could begin at West End on the steamer *Heroine* at 9:00 in the morning. Captain Boyle would steer the boat to the wharf in Mandeville, where one first glanced Colomes Hotel (to the right of the landing) and Frapart's (to the left). After partaking of food, drinks, perhaps a swim in the lake or various other entertainments, a return to the dock at 6:00 in the evening would result (after a stop at Lewisburg to pick up passengers) in reaching the city at the foot of Canal Street via the railway around 9:00 p.m.

Arceneaux's/Bechac's/Lake House

Paul Arceneaux opened Arceneaux's Casino Restaurant in 1880, but through the years, under Arceneaux's ownership, it was known as "Paul Arceneaux's Exchange" (where a lively 1883 Bastille Day celebration was held), "Paul's Exchange" in 1888 (when it was set amid forty oak trees), then simply as "The Casino" in 1902 (when Arceneaux celebrated his twenty-second year there).

It was headquarters for all sorts of revelry on the beach. An 1888 reception for the Morgan Fire Company No. 3 of Algiers included dinner for sixty at the Crescent Hotel and dancing on the platform at "Paul's." In 1893, its single electric lantern out front illuminated two beachfront blocks. In 1897, Mandeville's tinsmith, Mr. H. Tissot, had an office there. An 1898 summer

Paul Arceneaux's Casino offered rooms, board and more in 1910. *Louisiana Digital Collection.*

flag ceremony included a blessing of the American flag, speeches, children singing patriotic tunes, a display of flags of all nations along the beach and the raising of Old Glory on a seventy-five-foot staff.

The early 1900s brought political rallies, parties, dances, celebrations, meetings, horse selling and more. In 1907, Arceneaux was the King of Mandeville Carnival. Two years later, in 1909, Paul Arceneaux died, and a firm named Zarish & Weaver took over. But its run was very short. In 1910, a succinct advertisement appeared for months announcing that the firm "has on this day [October 29] been dissolved."

BECHAC FAMILY

French Pyrenees native Albert "Denis" Bechacq came to New Orleans as a child in 1852. His earliest work was as a waiter. He became a saloonkeeper in Milneburg and on Bourbon Street. After dropping the "q" from his name, he opened a restaurant at 19 Union Street in New Orleans on New Year's Eve 1869. It served breakfast and stayed open until after the theater crowd left. Private parlors allowed seating for between six and thirty-six diners.

Three generations of the Bechac family. *tammanyfamily.blogspot.com.*

In 1885, the establishment named Denis' Restaurant opened in Mandeville as the first of five generations of Bechac businesses there. In 1893, Denis Bechac was the lessee of Frapart's Hotel and Restaurant. Albert Denis Bechac died in 1897 at age fifty-five. The Bechacs appear to have opened their business at 2925 Lakeshore Drive in 1910 and called it "The Casino." In 1912, A.D. Paggio, promototer of the Casino, announced that a large dancing platform, bathhouses, a pavilion on the water, refreshment stands, a restaurant and accommodations for women and children on picnics were available at no cost. He also promised the coming of a wharf for yachts.

A 1913 sheriff's sale offered the Mandeville Casino, wharf and dancing pavilion. In 1914, the Reed and Bechac saloon stood near Girod Street. In 1915, Bechac and Mugnier sought a permit to continue the operation of a café and saloon there; the barroom was in an annex of the Mugnier Hotel. In 1918, the Mugniers sold a half share of their property to Albert and Dominica Bechac, who later acquired the remainder from them. The Bechacs then converted the upstairs of the Casino into a hotel. Albert Bechac and Company now owned the entire block bounded by the lake and Girod, Claiborne and Lafitte Streets. It was almost lost to a 1920 scheduled sheriff's sale, but the family resolved the matter prior to that event.

A 1921 *Times-Picayune* article tells us that not only did John James Audubon live at Bechac's "for many years" and that Bernard Marigny entertained there lavishly (neither is true), but also that boxer Pal Moran named it "one of the most famous eating places in the ozone belt." Moran liked it so much that he recommended it to fellow pugilists Martin Burke, Ashton Donza, Pete Herman, Red Dolan, Frankie Faren, Douglas Lee and more. They began training at the Casino when the upstairs was converted into a training center complete with punching bags, pulleys and an area for shadow boxing. In the side yard, in the sand, under a large magnolia tree, a boxing ring was placed. Bechac's Casino became one of the most famous training camps in the South, popular as such into the 1930s.

Albert Bechac ran the house while his wife did the cooking. In 1938, second-generation Denis spotted young William "Buster" Bivins on the lake crabbing and shrimping. He offered him a job cleaning out the property's "old plantation house" (the property was still a working farm with cows for milk and butter). Soon after, Bivins began working in the restaurant and then he became a waiter—well known and beloved. Bivens died at the age of seventy-three, having worked at Bechac's for forty-five years.

Albert "Bubber" Moise Bechac took over after his father died in 1946. Bubber passed away in 1968, leaving the legacy to his son A. Denis, who

Bechac's Restaurant in the 1970s. *tammanyfamily.blogspot.com.*

operated the business with his wife, Margherita. They restored the building to its original design and opened the upper porch for dining.

In 1967, waiter George Anderson died after fifty-five years at the restaurant. In 1980, waiter Norman Gainey retired after fifty-five years in service there. (His mother was the cook for thirty years.) Salad maker/pantry keeper Violet Cryer had been employed for twenty years in 1980. When waiters were still wearing formal black bowties and pants and gold jackets with black lapels, in 1983, writer Walker Percy dined there weekly. Joseph "Joe" Honore (age sixty-four) had been waiting tables for twenty years, having started out washing glasses behind the bar at age ten.

After four generations, the Bechacs ended their stand on Lakeshore Drive when Denis and Margherita retired in 1990 and leased the building. Shortly thereafter it became Pat Gallagher's redecorated Camelia Beach House (1990–93), named for the steamer. However, the Bechacs came back, this time for the fifth generation in 1993, when Denis and Margherita's sons Denis and Andrew and daughter Gina took over, using the family's same basic menu with new seasonal dishes.

Alex Patout tried his hand here in 2002 with his Louisiana Kitchen, but, shortly before Hurricane Katrina, a kitchen fire destroyed the dining room, with subsequent water damage in the mahogany-topped cinderblock bar. The building was restored. In 2008, Vickey Bayley and Cayman Sinclair opened it as the the Lakehouse. Since 2014, Sinclair has solely owned the business, which, at the time of this writing, is called the Lakehouse, at 2025 Lakeshore Drive.

Frapart House / Rest-A-While

The lovely Creole Cottage at 2129 Lakeshore Drive (west of Lafitte Street) was built in 1879 as the Frapart House and Restaurant. George Edmond Frapart, a native of Bordeaux, France, and his wife, Rosy Levy, managed the place, which was popular with New Orleanians. It had a large dance hall, restaurant, nice rooms and cool summer breezes. Prior to taking on his hotel venture, Frapart had managed the restaurant on the steamer *New Camelia*.

One account of Frapart's, in 1885, describes an artesian well that pumped a gallon of water every nine seconds, gas lighting, a chicken yard with hundreds of fryers, a turtle basin and a dinner of fried croakers.

In 1893, Frapart departed for Baton Rouge to manage the Verandah Hotel. He put the business on the market for sale or lease as a furnished hotel or residence with five cottages (three of which survive today). Denis Bechac secured the lease and offered special rates for boarders. In 1894, Frappart lost the property to creditors, and it came into ownership of the Mugniers, who sold it to Douglas S.M. Anderson and his wife. Mr. and Mrs. Sidney Story, he of New Orleans's Storyville fame, were guests there in 1894. An 1899 survey shows that the 180-by-506-foot property could house thirty to forty people.

A 1906 photograph of Rest-A-While. *tammanyfamily.blogspot.com.*

In 1905, Mrs. Anderson donated the property (in memory of her parents, Mr. and Mrs. James T. Rodd) to the Louisiana Branch of the New York–based International Order of the King's Daughters and Sons, a interdenominational Christian charitable organization that opened the complex as the Rest Awhile, a retreat for poor single mothers, their children and orphans.

Rest Awhile (later called "Rest-A-While") was dedicated on April 29, 1905, as, of course, "a home where the needy may rest for a while," where they could fish, swim, go boating and enjoy picnics under the oaks and pecans in the surrounding grove. In years to come, the children would have a goat as their mascot.

The main house, named the Margaret Rodd Memorial, had ten bedrooms, a dining room, a bathroom, a sitting room, a library and a reading room. A cottage named the James T. Rodd Memorial comprised four rooms, a hall and a kitchen. Each room was furnished with a bed, a washstand, a dresser, a bureau and two chairs. The Anderson home was adjacent to the main house.

In 1916, a central hall cottage was dedicated and named in honor of Sophie B. Wright. Built by the Order of the King's Daughters and Sons, it still exists at 2122 Claiborne Street. Wright, a state secretary and national officer in the organization, died in 1912 after having been instrumental in raising funds (she alone had raised $10,000) for its charitable endowment, which was also named for her in 1915. For the cottage dedication, the organization's convention delegates arrived by steamer from Spanish Fort after having taken the train from the Rampart station on Canal Street in New Orleans.

On adjacent property is the Dorothea Nolte Memorial Cottage, given to the Daughters and dedicated to the memory of the daughter of Dr. and Mrs. Arthur Nolte, who died in 1913 at age fifteen. The oldest remaining structure from the Rest Awhile is the Creole-style Fayssoux-Hadden Memorial Cottage, constructed around 1850 on adjacent property purchased by the organization. It was furnished by the family of Mrs. L.F. Hadden in her memory as an extremely active member of the charity.

The facility was later used to host youth groups, seniors and charitable organizations until Hurricane Katrina, after which it stood vacant. The Daughters, with a dwindling membership, could no longer afford to keep Rest Awhile, although the local chapter of King's Daughters and Sons sold its New Orleans property to provide money to stabilize the large building's foundation with steel support pillars and to repair its roof. In 2014, Mandeville resident Barrett McGuire purchased Rest Awhile for $750,000 with plans to convert it into a restaurant and tavern complex.

Mugnier's Hotel / St. Tammany Hotel

Between 1849 and 1850, Pierre D. Poutz built a cottage on Lakeshore Drive at Lafitte Street. Poutz, a New Orleans–based cotton buyer, purchased Fontainebleau three years later. Bernard Marigny owned and occupied the home from 1860 until his death in 1868 at age eighty. Here Marigny entertained guests, spent much time in his final years and visited six weeks before passing away.

Some time before 1879, it was used by François Colomes as a hotel and restaurant—said to be the sole hotel in Mandeville in 1880. French-born Colomes, who came to Louisiana in 1821, became a proprietor of Lucien Boudro's in Milneburg in 1852. During the Civil War, he opened the Carondelet Hotel in Spanish Fort until Federal troops pillaged it,

Undated photograph of Mugnier's Hotel. *Louisiana Digital Collection.*

leaving him penniless. He rebuilt his finances at the northshore hotel, which remained under the Colomes name until 1889.

Reportedly, in 1888, Marquis G.P. de Marigny (aka de Carabal, Bernard's grandson) bought Colomes Hotel from J.H. Lafferanderie with plans to renovate it and rename it the Crescent Hotel/Hall. It was a lively place, with a bathhouse and lovely tree-laden gardens that hosted balls and other lavish events.

In June 1898, family patriarch Joseph Mugnier celebrated his seventy-seventh birthday there, the year it was also put up for sale. It was again on the market in 1901. An April 4, 1902 *Times-Picayune* article described the hotel as "old" and "established" and the Mugnier family who hosted guests there as the only hoteliers in Mandeville.

A. Gustave (Gus) was the hotel manager, and his brother Henry, as chef, ran a large kitchen along with his wife, Theresa Martin. Henry's son Michel played the piano and sang for guests while they danced. Sister Jennie "looks after the ladies" (she also received guests at the *New Camelia* steamboat landing). Patriarch Joseph was said to be "a very entertaining gentleman," while "Aunt Carrie, an old-time 'mammy'…comes to see if you want fire on the cool mornings, and to bring you coffee before you are out of bed. She is always solicitous for your comfort and welfare." The article also states that the Mugniers "have been here now eleven years" (since 1881).

The main two-story building was 150 feet long with porches on both floors. The grounds included three cottages and a garden of roses, lilies, flowering vines and fountains. There were seven cottages in an annex with total hotel accommodations for two hundred guests. The Mugniers lived in a two-story house in the rear. A 1,500-foot wharf out front accommodated steamer landings at no cost. Joseph passed away in 1910 at age eighty-nine.

In 1915, the Bechac & Mugnier barroom was located in an annex to the hotel, just off the dining room. In 1918, the hotel was for sale with the following description: over fifty furnished rooms, a two-hundred-seat dining room, gardens and fruit and pecan trees on a 175-by-250-foot piece of property. "Established in 1885," read the advertisement.

For many years (since at least the early 1900s), the story was told that when the future king of France, Louis Philippe, visited Louisiana in 1798, he was entertained by Bernard Marigny (some said it was his father, as Bernard was thirteen years old at the time) and stayed at the Marignys' summer home. The bed and all furnishings he used were said to have been left in the room

FOR SALE ·

The Original Louis XIV (King of France)
Hand Carved Mahogany Bed and Dresser

which was used by His Majesty during his visit to Louisiana. Also other massive antique beds in black walnut and mahogany.

Address H. and G. Mugnier
Mugnier Hotel, Mandeville, La.

The future king allegedly slept here. A November 2, 1919 advertisement. Times-Picayune.

where he stayed (which, of course, was available and for guests). Because Bernard Marigny did not purchase an iota of St. Tammany property until 1829, this story is pure folklore. However, a November 2, 1919 advertisement offered the alleged bed and dresser for sale by the Mugniers at their hotel. It apparently did not sell; in 1949, Mike Mugnier again offered it for sale.

In the 1920s, the hotel was described as a "delightful summer resort" serving French cuisine and featuring boating, fishing, bathing and private bathhouses on the beach for guests. The Mugniers were still in management, and the cost was $2.50 per day on the American plan (breakfast, lunch and dinner included).

In 1922, Joseph Pugh, husband of Jennie Mugnier, bought it but put it up for sale, stating that, as owner and manager, he had other business interests demanding his attention. In 1923, the Mugniers advertised a "new confectionary" serving, among other delicacies, soft-shell crab sandwiches. The family remained there until at least 1924, when Pugh (who was then secretary-treasurer of the new St. Tammany Yacht Club) released a plan that would convert Mugnier's into the mammoth St. Tammany Hotel. The Colonial design left the historic building unrecognizable.

Pugh and associates hired architect R.S. Soule to enlarge the structure to sixty-five rooms with private baths accommodating two hundred guests on 150 feet of lake frontage. "A hotel where the South was at its best" would be managed by Jennie's nephew. Her family's hotel now offered not only music and dancing and wide verandas, but also sixty screened rooms, private

Hotel St. Tammany in an undated photograph. *tammanyfamily.blogspot.com*.

baths, telephones and a two-hundred-seat dining room. Its formal opening was celebrated on April 24, 1925. Don J. Thomas was the manager, while W.L. Brown served as president of the firm, operating the "new" hotel under the American plan. They hosted Saturday Supper Dances (reportedly frequented by many New Orleanians) with Rene Soloman's orchestra. By 1927, Pugh was the parish engineer and president of the Mandeville Chamber of Commerce.

With a reported $1 million in backing, the Louisiana Academy of Motion Picture Arts bought the hotel in 1928 with plans to convert it into classrooms, dormitories and studios to be leased to motion picture producers. Here, actors and technicians would live and be trained, producing three or more movies per year "with the historical background of the South." But the hotel would also remain open for tourist stays.

Academy president Ernest Shipman also had plans for offices in New Orleans. A Hollywood director and choreographer were dispatched to Mandeville. Victor Fleming was engaged by the Louisiana Academy in 1929 when he was in the process of preparing a production schedule. Ten years later, Fleming would direct *Gone with the Wind* and *The Wizard of Oz*.

Also in the works was the purchase of the Canadian rum-running schooner *I'm Alone* as a floating studio, which was agreeable to its infamous captain, John T. Randell. At a welcoming celebration hosted by the Association of Commerce, a reported 1,500 people came from Tangipahoa, Washington and St. Tammany Parishes to see local talent who might become movie stars on display and to view a seven-reel silent motion picture, *Sky Pilot*. In 1929, the *Times-Picayune* reported, "Mandeville people are highly enthusiastic over the Academy," which would be a "tourist magnet." The grand plans of the academy apparently did not pan out.

In 1936, the hotel was operating as the Alva and was purchased by Mr. and Mrs. O.P. Hall. For sale again in 1944, it was bought in 1946 by Mr. and Mrs. Oscar M. Moroy. A 1947 advertisement boasted of the "most beautiful cocktail lounge in the Florida Parishes" while offering furnished rental apartments by day, week or month. In 1948, it was again on the market, a result of the owner retiring. New managers came in 1949, and in 1950, a totally renovated complex "only 1 hour and 15 minutes from New Orleans on paved highway" was for sale.

Again for sale in 1953 (still as the Alva Hotel), in 1958, it was renamed the Georgian Manor Hotel, owned by Mr. and Mrs. Doyce R. Clark. The following year, the Clarks had a dispute with the Town of Mandville over their liquor license, and so, in 1959, the old place was for sale, rent or lease—fifty-seven rooms, thirty-seven baths, a "charming" dining room and a "unique cocktail lounge." At this time, it welcomed retirees to lodge at monthly rates, which included two meals a day.

In 1964, state fire marshal Milton Stire ordered its complete demolition. In the late 1990s, Chateau De Mugnier Condominiums took its place at 2075 Lakeshore Drive.

The Mandeville shoreline in 1907. *tammanyfamily.blogspot.com.*

Audubon Hotel

Opening some time before 1909, the two-story, white-columned, nineteen-room Audubon Hotel facing the lake welcomed cool breezes on its upper and lower porches overlooking lovely old oak trees. Very popular in the 1920s, it was fully screened by 1928 and equipped with running water in each room and an "excellent table" at a cost of twelve dollars. By 1946, it was owned by James F. Brandin, who advertised in 1948 that it was open year-round with attic fans in each room, innerspring mattresses, venetian blinds, tiled private baths and a deep freeze. He also touted the paved road to Fontainebleau State Park as well as the close proximity to the proposed causeway.

Mrs. R.S. Wolfson owned the Audubon in 1951, offering horseback riding in addition to the usual fishing and swimming. In 1957, it was for sale: "15 rooms with baths, lobby, reading room, large upper and lower porch, huge kitchen, laundry room. Must sell to settle estate." It was purchased by Mr. and Mrs. Albert Petrie in 1958. At that time, Albert Petrie stated that the hotel was fifty years old and that the cook he retained had twenty years' experience. In 1960, Petrie offered a free stay at the hotel to anyone who visited if their stay resulted in the purchase of St. Tammany property from his company, A.B. Petrie Realty Co. In 1969, it was purchased by Dr. and Mrs. Edward Mernin, who made it a home for their twelve children. Nine years later, the building was completely destroyed in a 1978 fire.

Undated Audubon Hotel photograph. *tammanyfamily.blogspot.com.*

JACKSON PARK

Opened around 1893, bounded by Coffee, Jefferson and Adair Streets, Jefferson Park was set back from the lakeshore near the *Camelia* landing. Owned by Jules Manaud, it hosted outdoor parties and picnics. An 80-by-100-foot platform could accommodate five hundred people under mossy oaks and magnolia trees. A dance pavilion sat on the lake side of the park. In 1894, a free ball was given every Sunday with music by the Mandeville String Band. In 1897, Manaud added a half-mile horse and bicycle racing track, baseball fields and a shooting gallery. After Manaud's death in 1906, the park and his home were put up for sale to settle his estate. It included a five-room lakefront cottage, a chicken house, a stable, a wine cellar and pecan and pear trees on a 100-by-250-foot property.

The park remained an entertainment venue until the mid-1930s. An example of the fun had there (and getting there) is the 1911 picnic of the local branch of the Metropolitan Life Insurance Company. Based in the Maison Blanche building in New Orleans, the day began with a parade down Canal Street to the tunes of the Maccabees's Band and a string orchestra. When they reached Barrone Street, the merrymakers boarded five chartered train cars for a ride out to Spanish Fort on the steamer *Louis Dolive*, where the dancing began. Upon arrival at Mandville, a second parade to the park was led by company leaders adorned in sashes and spangles. Speeches were made by Mandeville's mayor, a Mr. Hartman, and others at the dancing pavilion. A cakewalk followed; then the games began. There was a fat man's race and a slim man's race, a ladies' needle-threading contest and a waltzing contest.

1900s

At the turn of the twentieth century, Mandeville came into its own as a playground for New Orleans's rich and an excursion destination for those not so wealthy. Now there were more hotels and restaurants along the lake and even more steamers from New Orleans: *Cape Charles*, *Susquehanna*, *Josie* and, later, *Reverie*. And there were more wharves for docking them. Eating, drinking and dancing to bands on the boats and in the bathhouses and pavilions were popular forms of entertainment.

For boaters, there was the Mandeville Yacht Club. The Lake View / Lakeview Hotel was located near Coffee Street prior to 1904 but was destroyed by a fire in 1914.

DUVALLE'S

Duvalle's properties included a bathhouse out over the lake, the Showboat (a bar and dance hall used by picnickers) and a lush garden—all on Lakeshore Drive some time before 1910. From 1910 to 1918, the St. Tammany and New Orleans Railway ran from Duvalle's steamboat dock to Abita Springs and Covington.

A major event there is represented by the three thousand people who attended the 1936 New Orleans Grocers' Association annual picnic. Some arrived via the steamer *Madisonville*, where they danced during both trips across the lake. Upon arrival, they were greeted at the landing by Dr. (and

Duvalle's Bath House pictured in an undated photograph. *Sidney Gale at tammanyfamily. blogspot.com.*

Mayor) R.B. Payne before parading to Duvalle's Garden to dance at the pavilion. Games and contests were enjoyed: the fat man's race was won by A.J. Ringenberg, the egg race winner was F.J. Schoenberger and Russell Kirst and Lynn Smith won the three-legged race. Famous New Orleans barkeeper Nick G. Castrogiovanni (co-owner of Nick's Big Train Bar on Tulane Avenue) was the picnic committee chair. Also in 1936, a weekend-long benefit for needy Mandeville citizens was held at Duvalle's. The themed Country Fair included a greased-pig contest, booths, a dance contest, floor shows and Christmas gifts.

MANDEVILLE INN

Originally the Welcome Hotel, which opened sometime before 1909, by 1915, it operated as the Mandeville Inn. Located two properties east of Mugnier's between Lafitte and Girod Streets, it contained a café, a saloon with an oyster bar, a pool hall and rooms operated by J.L. Reed.

This six-foot, seven-inch, 160-pound tarpon was caught near the Mandeville Inn around 1915. *tammanyfamily.blogspot.com.*

1910s

From 1915 to 1921, a concrete seawall was constructed and a dance pavilion added. Mrs. J.M. Favaron operated a boardinghouse in summer and provided food for excursion visitors. Mrs. A.M. Beret owned Bert's House, open all year as a boardinghouse managed by F.E. Collet. By 1916, the Hip Theater entertained with bands and dances.

COMMERCIAL/CENTRAL HOTEL

In 1919, the Commercial Hotel near the depot was leased, refitted with "modern conveniences" and renamed the Central Hotel under the management of Mrs. J. Coltora, who had run the Commercial, which had touted its proximity to the courthouse, post office, picture show, garages and livery. Meals and a short-order menu were served, often to jury members who were also housed in the hotel. That same year, the St. Tammany Parish Medical Society convened here.

1920s

The steamer *Reverie* was running daily from Madisonville to Mandeville to West End by 1922. By the mid-1920s, auto ferries from West End transferred cars (in about two hours) to Mandeville, where three long wharves awaited them. In 1928, the completion of the first automobile bridge connecting New Orleans to the North Shore rang the death knell for the steamboat era.

ST. TAMMANY YACHT CLUB AT MANDEVILLE

Organized in 1923 by Henry Pruden with plans to build a clubhouse, this boating club held its first regatta and water carnival that year with a bathing review, swimming races, footraces, a diving exhibition and more. Its 1924 regatta was headquartered at Elk's Park and Pavilion (in the same block as the Tammany Hotel). In 1928, its harbor was at Bayou Castine.

The club faded from existence, but a new one, chartered in 1980 and named Tammany Yacht Club, was established in Slidell.

HARBOR INN

Located at the St. Tammany Steamer Auto Ferry dock, the Harbor Inn opened around 1925, serving sandwiches, cold drinks, coffee and the like at its tables or to cars parked in its lot. Its proprietors were E.H. Baudot and B. Cusach.

1930s

From 1938 to 1940, the federal Works Progress Administration built sidewalks and steps along the shoreline. The 1938 New Orleans City Guide describes Mandeville as a place to enjoy "fishing, swimming, and boating where…many summer cottages are maintained here. There are good hotels and several boarding-houses; cottages may be rented."

A 1929 photograph of the Victory Bath House, whose proprietor was Mr. Vulliet. *tammanyfamily.blogspot.com.*

Cliff's on the Beach

Built by Cliff Glockner "On the Beach" in the early 1930s, this establishment was originally a low-slung, commercial-style, stucco-fronted bar and restaurant with a neon sign typical of the era. In the 1940s, Cliff's also had a swimming pier. In the early 1950s, Glockner added eleven air-conditioned brick motel units to his 67-by-250-foot beach property, which included his home. In 1956, when T.J. "Brother" LeCompte was the bartender, James Henderson caught a Lake Pontchartrain record trout weighing eight pounds, four ounces at Cliff's dock.

Glockner passed away in 1981. Blaise P. Bourcq Sr. was the proprietor for a time. Doris and Fredrick Reppel bought the business and the property in 1983. They renamed it Rip's and kept it going for three decades. The Reppels faced what some locals called the most rain in fifty-nine years when Hurricane Georges, in 1998, created a three-foot storm surge that pushed about five inches of water into the building.

Roslyn and Clay Prieto bought Rip's at 1917 Lakeshore Drive in 2002. After a sixty-seven-day, $200,000 renovation that included additional windows for a better lake view, they began their new business. Clay made the roux, boiled the seafood and smoked the prime rib; Roslyn ran the kitchen. One week later, Tropical Storm Isadore swept eighteen inches of mud, sand and water into the place. They swept and shoveled it out, only to face a similar situation the following week when Hurricane Lily paid a visit to Lakeshore Drive, leaving about eight inches of muck in its wake. Then there was Bill, the tropical storm that, in 2003, washed water into the dining room while people were unknowingly eating and drinking. Again, the Prietos prevailed, repaired and rebuilt.

And then there was Katrina, which washed their contents five blocks back from the shore while leaving the interior gutted by the surge. Of course, they rebuilt, this time atop 17-foot pilings beginning in January 2006. They reopened yet again in October of that year with a 3,300-square-foot bar and restaurant able to accommodate seven hundred customers. When, in 2012, Hurricane Isaac left water on Lakeshore Drive more than 6 feet deep, Rip's was high and dry. It bears no resemblance to the old Cliff's on the Beach, but it stands as a testament to how accomplished many locals are at literally riding out the storms.

Lewisburg

Named for Judge Joshua Lewis, the community was established in 1834, the same year as Mandeville. It is noted for its beautiful ancient oak trees, most notably the 1,500-year-old Seven Sisters Oak—the largest certified southern live-oak tree, measuring 38.9 feet in circumference. Like Mandeville, Lewisburg was a favorite lakeshore getaway for wealthy New Orleanians, some of whom built fine vacation homes there. But Lewisburg never developed as a hotel resort. Technically, now within the municipality of Mandeville, it was cut off from the busier section of town by the Causeway bridge.

As early as 1841, the steamer *Walker* made its way to Lewisburg. Then came the U.S. Mail steamers *Undine* and *Corrine* in 1845, the mailboats *Hempstead* and *Delaware* in 1847, the *Olivia* in 1848 and, the following year, the *Lenora*. All of them ran from the Pontchartrain Railroad Depot in Milneburg. An 1856 storm destroyed the Lewisburg wharf along with seven of nine bathhouses. (The wharf was rebuilt.)

Hope for a Railroad

The Mandeville and Sulphur Springs Railroad was incorporated in 1868 to run across the lake from Lewisburg to Bienville Street in New Orleans. Two years later, the line became the New Orleans and Northeastern Railroad. In 1876, the Louisiana State House of Representatives Bill No. 157, titled "An Act to Incorporate the Lewisburg Wharf Company," was approved. J.F. Carter was contracted in 1878 to construct a wharf at Lewisburg, 940 feet into the lake, to be used to unload boats laden with iron rails and also to eventually serve as the first section of the bridge/trestle. A depot with a pier extending into the lake was constructed at Lewisburg (at the approximate location of the Lake Pontchartrain Causeway).

In 1878, Carter sued for work, materials and interest for the construction of the wharf. By 1880, the railroad still was unbuilt, and in 1881, right-of-way problems through New Orleans resulted in a change to the planned route, whereby the road would cross the lake from the southshore from Alligator Bayou (near or at Kenner). Then plans changed again: from Bayou Bon Fouca, then again from Pointe Aux Herbes and again to near the Pontchartrain Railroad's lake-end wharf. The train's final/existing route takes it across the lake from near Eden Isles and through the Bayou Sauvage National Wildlife preserve, then along the New Orleans lakeshore (through Little Woods and along Hayne Boulevard) and over the Industrial Canal to Peoples Avenue and finally to Press Street. Its first run was made on October 15, 1883. The pilings at Lewisburg and in Kenner remained for years afterward.

1880s–1920s

Residents of Lewisburg in 1881 included Homus Frederick, who owned seven acres, as well as B.B. Robert, Goody Smith, Mrs. M.M. Stagg, Henry Tricou, L. Valton and N. Vallon. By 1883, the little town could boast of having its own doctor and drugstore, school, churches, grocery stores, lodgings and telephone service. A dozen or so homes now line its shore.

In 1883, Jules B. Herbelin planted 7,000 mulberry trees for his plan to establish a silk cocoonery and factory at Lewisburg. The following year, he planned to clear a forest to plant 25,000 more trees and employ girls and women to spin silk. In 1886, he lost his assets to creditors.

Lakeview Poultry Farm had a three-hundred-square-foot chicken house in 1884. Citizens contributed $1,000 for building a new wharf, which was completed in 1884. The *New Camelia* began daily service to Lewisburg, and C.E. Black purchased two properties.

In 1910, residents included Isabelle David and Mr. Jones, owner of the Lewisburg Sawmill. The next year, the steamer *Louis Dolive* was running from Spanish Fort. By 1919, the Poitevant and Farve sawmill near the town kept the wharf busy, and by 1922, the company constructed a pavilion. Mr. and Mrs. Frank B. Haynes (of the Lake Shore Land Company) bought a grand old house surrounded by oaks in 1927.

CAMP ONWARD (LEWISBURG)

In the late 1800s, Trinity Episcopal Church in New Orleans established a free kindergarten mission school for the Irish Channel's underserved girls as well as English classes for their immigrant mothers. For this, they found a large brick building on Tchoupitoulas Street and called it Kingsley House.

The mission was transformed into a Settlement House (the first in the South), where middle-class adults lived amid the poor to educate and offer assistance in achieving self-sufficiency and social consciousness. From this humble beginning grew an organization that would provide the city's first free clinic (in 1903), first playground (1904) and first vacation school. It was a haven from idleness on tough city streets.

In 1904, Eleanor McMain created the virtual "City of Onward" (aka "Onward City"), where the children in the vacation school governed themselves. She served as the "Lawyer for the Defense" of any child who broke "the rules" of kindness and consideration for others enacted by the students. Children served as mayor, police (and chief thereof) and heads of various committees composed of fellow students.

In 1909, McMain, with Harriet Barton, organized Camp Onward and arranged for the use of beach property in Lewisburg. In July of that year, the steamer *Ozona* (compliments of the Holton Lumber Company) transported thirty-four girls, one boy and some parents from its dock at West End to the first of several two-week sessions on the beach. Older children helped the mothers in caring for the youngest among them. A session for boys soon followed.

Almost all work was done by the campers: pitching tents for the boys' sleeping quarters, dressing room and bathroom; setting up cots and

Eleanor McMain is third from the right in this 1909 photograph. *Louisiana Digital Library.*

Camp Onward sleeping porch. *Kingsley House.*

mosquito bars on the wraparound porch, where the girls and adults bedded down; household chores; chopping wood for cooking and campfires; sewing dishtowels, mailbags and yellow pillows embroidered in red with "Camp Onward, Lewisburg."

The City of Onward concept prevailed at the camp, where the children appointed officials and served on various bodies and committees. The Department of Health limed the latrines. The Civics Committee kept all things tidy. The Water Works monitored the well house and provided potable water. The Improvement Commission decorated the camp with ferns and flowers picked during exploring expeditions. The Police Department enforced the rules.

Camp Onward's constitution, also written by the children, officially mandated that their Lewisburg grounds be named the Republic of Onward and that it be self-governing, with equal rights and a voice for all. The purpose of the government, as stated, was to make members happy and keep them well. "Any citizen not wishing to take his [her] punishment when he [she] deserves it, will have the privilege of leaving The Republic, if he [she] so desires" stated one of the rules. Another mandated that a citizen must never use anything not belonging to him or her without permission from the owner. But when a skiff drifted near ten boys swimming, they could not resist paddling it out to deeper water to use as a diving platform. "The Police" nabbed them and brought them in. Most were community leaders who pleaded guilty to all charges and sentenced themselves to spend half a day in bed wearing nightgowns. This would result in them missing a sailboat excursion. The skiff owner felt that the punishment was too harsh for the crime. A few hours after their sentence was partially served, the boys begged Miss McMain, "Can't you beat us?" instead of missing the fun. The governing authorities prevailed, and the sentence was served in full.

A typical day at Camp Onward ended with a meeting on the porch of the clubhouse for committee reports, followed by storytelling and singing around the piano in the central hall or around a campfire on the beach. A day began with rising at 6:00 a.m., breakfast, committee work until 9:00, followed by swimming, exploring the woods or simply relaxing. At 12:30, the children had lunch, then played games or sewed before bathing in preparation for dinner (which might be a fish fry) on the back porch, followed by the meetings. Special activities included dances, costume parties, broom drills and sailboat trips to Mandeville and the Tchefuncte River. All this for a fifty-cent per-camper fee paid in coins earned by each child, supplemented by five dollars donated by a generous New Orleanian.

Taking a dip in the lake. *Kingsley House.*

In late September, storm-driven water threatened all who huddled together in the clubhouse. When its contents began floating, McMain led the children and adults through high winds and surging waves to the storehouse with its brick foundation. They huddled there for hours, some thirty people of all ages. Near midnight, when it, too, became wave-beaten and flooded, McMain instructed older children to cling to plank rafts while the women hoisted the youngest on their shoulders and carried them in neck-deep surging waters to the higher ground of townspeople's homes. All Camp Onward structures were washed away by the six-and-a-half-foot surge, with the exception of the storehouse. The following morning, a camp was set up on the grounds of a nearby unused residence. Food was salvaged from the higher shelves of the storehouse. Neighbors sent over morning coffee, homemade bread and other needed goods. Four days after the storm, all returned home on the steamer *Expert*. The youngest camper was one and a half years old, the oldest, fourteen. Along with the kindness and help from the good people of Lewisburg, a young man, sixteen-year-old Ferdinand Foster, was highly lauded for bravery and help in saving the children during the height of the storm.

The following summer, the camp moved to DeBuys, Mississippi. Eleanor Laura McMain served at Kingsly House untiringly for thirty-three years. In 1918, she was awarded one of the city's highest honors, the *Times-Picayune* Loving Cup, for community service. Before her death in 1934, a public school was named in her honor. McMain was well known and loved by New Orleanians for her work in the enactment of child-labor legislation, community health laws and the establishment of a citywide recreational system, vocational training and night schools.

6

THE WESTERN SHORE

A 1854 description of a ride from New Orleans to this area on the New Orleans, Jackson and Great Northern Railroad (aka the "Great Northern") gives us a glimpse of the terrain at that time. The train ran westerly for fifty minutes, mostly though open marshy plains filled with grasses, reeds and palmettos, then into what remained of cypress forests that had already been thinned for lumber. There was a stop in the "new town" of Kenner (about ten miles from the city), which comprised four or five houses. The train continued with a view of land planted with corn and sugarcane, then passed the three Kenner family plantations, workhouses and cattle. Nearing the lake, steamboats came into view, then the train went onward through a prairie of multicolored wild cotton/hibiscus flowers, across Bayou La Branche and to its station (twenty miles from New Orleans), about one-quarter mile from the lake. The bayou was eighteen feet deep, and the old bathhouses and all the rest were relics. But the area was still popular for hunting and fishing. The train continued onward to Frenier and Manchac.

By 1869, the railroad ran excursions every Sunday to Magnolia, Mississippi, and back to New Orleans on Monday. The train made stops at Kenner, Frenier, Manchac, Ponchatoula, Tickfaw, Amite, Tangipaho and Osyka. The Great Northern was acquired by the Illinois Central Railroad in 1883.

Tangipahoa, St. John the Baptist and St. Charles Parishes hug the western shore of Lake Pontchartrain. *1890 U.S. Geological Survey.*

TANGIPAHOA PARISH

Jones Island

A 1913 *Times-Picayune* article described Jones Island as a place that "lies somewhere in the 'never was' of space....The uninitiated might as well try to find the Isles of Hesperides, or hunt out the seas where King Rex spends 363 days of each year." But the Jones Island Pleasure Club had been there annually for the past four years. From the New Basin Canal, club members traversed on two Jahncke-built barges (Jahnckes were club members) pulled by a tugboat into Pass Manchac, then into Lake Maurepas to their "Kingdom of Jones Island." They had breakfast onboard along the way and a "magnificent" celebratory dinner for the election of officers. The officers included well-known New Orleans businessmen, including P.J. McMahon (elected chief of police) and florist Harry Papworth (commissioner of agriculture).

This raucous group of jesters first made their way to their island in 1911 and then yearly after. At a 1913 meeting, the club viewed motion pictures

141

MEMBERS OF THE JONES ISLAND PLEASURE CLUB WHO GIVE AN EXCURSION YEARLY TO JONES ISLAND NEAR MANCHAC LA.

The 1912 Jones Island Pleasure Club annual excursion via the steamer *Claribel*.
Daily Picayune.

of the island. In 1915, the club described its annual meeting as a fishing excursion and chartered the *New Camelia*. It (along with the members) ran aground, stuck on a shell bar for three hours, three miles from Pass Manchac. When finally freed, the two hundred men aboard found themselves aground for a second time. Consequently, the "refreshments were served in abundance," and all was well with most members. This was their last trip to Jones Island; thereafter, they traveled on the Mississippi River to various outposts.

Manchac

As early as 1852, the steamer *Ophelia* ran to Manchac near the Pass Manchac Lighthouse, which was surrounded by a breakwater. In 1854, there were steamboat excursions to Pass Manchac and Lake Maurepas. The first Great Northern fishing excursion to Manchac via train was offered in 1893. In 1919, the Illinois Central Railroad began offering fishing excursions, leaving New Orleans at 2:15 a.m. and 6:30 a.m. In the 1930s, the area was a popular fishing and hunting ground, where boats, guides and accommodations could be found and seafood was sold.

St. John the Baptist Parish

Failed Plan

In the March 6, 1914 *Times-Picayune*, a page-twelve article announced "Gigantic Plan Forming to Establish Magnificent Resort on Pontchartrain Shores." This plan included a thirty-one-mile seawall, with reclaimed land behind it, and a "great highway" five hundred, or even two thousand, feet from the current shoreline between West End and Ruddock. New Orleans had recently built a seawall from the New Basin Canal to the Jefferson Parish line and created West End Park on reclaimed land, so the proposed "great highway" would connect to it. Electric streetcars would whisk along its neutral grounds, "a magnificent resort hotel" would be built and twenty thousand visitors yearly would partake of these glories. The plan, it was said, would surpass the magnificence of Chicago's Lake (Michigan) Shore Drive. This scheme was the first hint of what would become the planned New Orleans–Hammond Highway, which was, also, never completed.

Frenier

Around 1850, German immigrant Martin Schlosser settled in a remote area of St. John the Baptist Parish on the far southwestern shore of the lake, where he grew excellent cabbage from seed brought from his homeland and made wood barrel staves. Members of his extended family soon joined him there and established their own cabbage farm. Their produce was shipped by boat to the New Orleans market.

In 1854, the Great Northern reached the settlement, allowing for their products to be easily shipped to distant markets, packed in barrels made by the Schlossers. Frenier cabbage and sauerkraut became known for their quality. By the 1880s, the surrounding area boomed with sawmills and the formation of the company town, Ruddock, as well as the little towns of La Branche, Wagram/Napton, De Sair and Galva.

A hurricane in 1909 caused 350 deaths (8 in Frenier) and much destruction. But it was the great hurricane of 1915 that abruptly ended the prosperity of this area. The towns were literally wiped off the map (with the exception of Ruddock, which still exists, primarily in name only).

In 1926, Dr. J.K. Small of New York Botanical Garden first identified the giant native *Sabal deeringianna* palmettos growing around the lake and swamps near LaPlace, at Frenier. Dr. Small proclaimed that these grew only in Louisiana on what was often called the "trembling prairies."

In 1927, S.T. Christina and John L. Lauricella, owners and developers of Frenier Beach and Estates, boasted in advertisements that "The Land Is High and Dry!," but at that time, only the unpaved Ory Cutoff road enabled drivers to reach the properties via Airline or Jefferson Highways near the Mississippi River. The developers also planned a $60,000 amusement park and dance hall / pavilion as well as a seawall. Beachfront properties stretched 100 feet along the shore and 1,100 feet back; a total of 754 building sites (most inland) were offered. A 140-foot-wide road with a neutral ground would run through the three-mile-long lakeside property.

Two years after promising the amusement park, Christina announced that a beach and dance pavilion would be ready to open in 1929. The dirt Ory Cutoff road was walkable but too derelict for most autos. Despite that, the Longino and Collins packinghouse company hosted a picnic for two hundred employees, including a bathing review of eight female employees—Thelma Tank won the tiara.

In the early 1930s, the enterprising developers added a pier and bathhouses on the "beach," which had little sand but was shaded with lovely oak and cypress trees, making it appealing as a place to picnic, hunt, fish and swim. It remained fairly popular when the accompanying photo captured a view of it in 1939.

In 1932, the Mystic Krewe, a carnival club of the United Ancient Order of Druids, chartered an Illinois Central train to Frenier, where they were provided a picnic with fishing, boating, bathing, games with prizes and dancing in the pavilion to the tunes of John Senac's W.W.L. Paramount Band.

During the 1930s, Mr. Keating managed the beach properties, which included Keating's Log Cabin Inn and Bathhouse, which provided accouterments for hunting deer, rabbit, squirrel and duck, as well as boat rentals. By 1936, the shoreline Hammond Highway was graveled from West End to Frenier, making access by automobiles much easier. (The road was not well maintained and gradually washed away.)

In 1937, the Benevolent Knights of America chartered the train then paraded to the picnic grounds led by Johnny DeDroit's band, which played all day. Tennis matches and baseball games were played. The Knights had such a good time at Frenier that they returned the following year.

In 1941, residents reported that the shoreline had partially washed away since the opening of the Bonnet Carré Spillway in 1937 and what

On December 18, 1927, with the promise of the New Orleans–Hammond Highway passing through, would-be developers promoted "Frenier Beach Estates." Times-Picayune.

Frenier Beach in 1939. *Louisiana Digital Library.*

remained was littered with driftwood. Locals also complained that saltwater intrusion from spillway runoff intermingled with brackish lake water was ruining crops and vegetation, so much so that their cattle were starving. The spillway was again opened in 1945 and 1950, likely leading to the demise and abandonment of Frenier Beach.

Some fifty-five years after its popularity waned, a public boat launch was built at Frenier in 1995. In recent times, at the end of Peavine Road off U.S. Highway 51, a small resettlement leaves Frenier with some camps, homes and restaurants.

St. Charles Parish

Bayou La Branche

The settlement of Bayou La Branche was located approximately at what is now Wetland Watchers Park (near the lake end of the spillway's Lower Guide Levee). In 1839, it was the terminus of the New Orleans and Nashville Railroad. In August of that year, the turnouts for the train were completed at both ends so that the engine could pull the cars in either direction. In September, there were fireworks and music at Bayou La Branche, hosted by Frederick Proctor (see chapter 7).

By 1841, the Bayou La Branche Hotel advertised its fine bar and restaurant, and the railroad made a Sunday stop there and three stops at Prairie Cottage (see chapter 7). Later in the year, advertisements touted "Bayou La Branch [sic]—Hyde Park" and informed the public that Speakman and Company had newly purchased it and was serving fish dinners, soft- and hard-shelled crabs and turtle soup. The company had made arrangements with the railroad, so it said, for trains to arrive on Wednesdays and Sundays.

All seemed well in 1842, when the train was running between Bayou La Branche, Prairie Cottage, Bath Tower (see chapter 7) and New Orleans. Then the railroad failed, and so did the resort, as the railway was the principal means of bringing visitors to it.

Long after the hotel resort was abandoned, in 1875, Louis Wire ran a hunting ranch and cabin at the bayou where he had been hunting and fishing for thirty years, bagging duck, snipe, partridges, squirrels and bullfrogs. In the early 1900s, the La Branche Hunting and Fishing Club provided refuge for outdoorsmen.

7

JEFFERSON PARISH

During the 1830s, the "Free State of Jefferson" cast a blind eye on illegal gaming and drinking. A few camps sprouted up along its shoreline—some homes, some "clubs" and some taverns. Some resorts also sprang up, but they have long since been replaced with suburban homes and businesses. It is difficult now to imagine Jefferson's shoreline terrain as "4 to 5 miles of marsh prairie bordered by solid ground supporting live-oak trees," as described in the 1880 U.S. Census Report.

PRAIRIE COTTAGE

In 1838, along what is now Metairie's Canal Street, the tracks of the New Orleans and Nashville Railroad headed straight out from New Orleans's Canal Street to the lakeshore between Bayou Labarre and Bayou Laurier. Bridges were built across Indian Bayou and Bayous Tchoupitoulas and Labarre. The train passed through the "town" of Bath (see later in this chapter) to the Prairie Cottage resort and onward to distant Bayou La Branche—five trips per day.

Prairie Cottage was a first-class resort on high ground near a beach. Built in the late 1830s, this endeavor was successful with its good restaurant, bar, family accommodation rooms, billiard rooms, pistol and rifle range, courts for quoit pitching (akin to horseshoes) and bathhouses. Named for its expansive

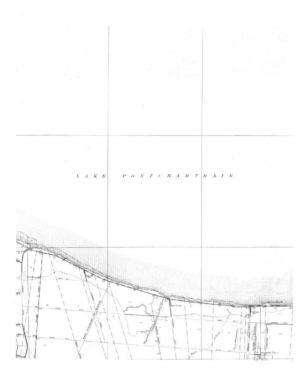

The Jefferson Parish Shore, 1937. *U.S. Geological Survey.*

greatest evils attending
ng, have arisen from the
tren have left the bosom
us taken the place and
a parent. This evil is
. The President is the
Professors and assistant
en of the pupils. In the
boys neither study, eat,
resence of a teacher.—
in successful operation
etween 20 and 30 pupils,
ructed by five teachers,
 two terms of 22 weeks
 first Monday of Octo-
t Monday of April.
cal year, for which the
ion, beds, bedding, fuel,
ring apparel, books and
l the French and Span
required, at an extra
per dozen, Books and
es; and $15 per term, of
nish.

many 23 ts1   Proprietor.

PRAIRIE COTTAGE.

This airy and pleasant watering place is
now open for the season, under conduction of
the subscribers. It is designed to keep up a
succession of attractive amusements during the summer, such as pistol and rifle shooting, sail boats, seine
fishing, quoit pitching, &c. Fish and chowder dinners will be served up regularly every Sunday.—
Parties to dinner during the week provided for at one
day's notice. Bathing accommodations ready at all
times. [june 3]   JOURDAN & KENT

ST GEORGE HOTEL

From Montgom
TRAVELLERS a
    daily line of fou
in connection with th
gomery Railroads, l
cities. This line p
Madison, Eatonton,
Zebulon, Greenville,
ta and Franklin to
over the Georgia, M
roads.
    With regard to the
be sufficient to state t
by any other; that t
good or better than t
through Georgia. E
render this line unex
petent and civil dri
horses.
Leave Augusta daily
    at Montgomery at t
ing after their dep
Leave Montgomery a
    rive in time to tak

September 14, 1841 advertisement for the Prairie Cottage. Daily Picayune.

view of the swamp prairie that was spread back from Metairie's lakeshore, it hosted popular regattas and pistol matches and provided sailboats, seine fishing and bathhouses. In 1839, the proprietor was Frederick Proctor, followed by persons named Jourdan and Kent in 1841, when a hot-air balloon race stirred excitement. Wagers were placed on the fastest, highest-flying and quickest balloon back to the ground.

In March 1842, the main building burned to the ground. The proprietors promised to rebuild, but the railroad went into foreclosure that same year and ceased running. At auction in 1842 were twenty-three miles of track, land (fifty feet from the center of the track), two locomotives, six passenger cars and the forty slaves who resided in a railroad car while building the tracks. With the failure of the railroad that brought city folk here, the resort was doomed in this pre-automobile age. Prairie Cottage was located approximately where today Edenborn Avenue runs to the lake.

Edgewater Club

When the Edgewater Club first sprouted up in the lake due east of what would become the Lake Pontchartrain Causeway is a mystery, but a June 1, 1934 *Times-Picayune* ad announced its season opening with the Steve Lewis Orchestra for "Dining, Dancing, Bathing." It was a camp built high on pilings along the Hammond Highway. When it was demolished in 1962, equipment, lumber, tables, chairs, a barback and even a cypress cistern were put up for sale. The building is long gone, but its pilings remain visible.

Town of Bath

In 1836, Henri Bonnabel purchased from Hypolite de Courval a half interest in twelve arpents (approximately 2,300 feet) along Metairie Road/Bayou, stretching from the river to the lake. As a condition of the transaction, a portion of the tract, 240 feet wide and 1,100 feet long, was reserved for a proposed railroad, which was later built.

They collaborated in laying out a "town" they named Bath, assigning the numbered street names we still use today, with the first street starting at the lake and counting up to Forty-Fourth Street at Metairie Road. Bonnabel and

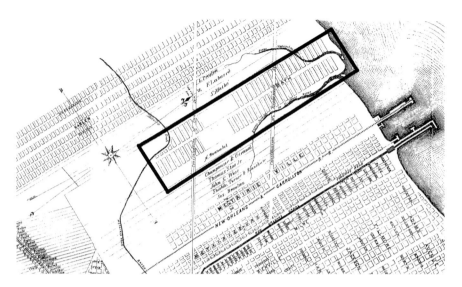

Author's overlay outlining the town of Bath on Gardner's 1867 City Directory map. *Gardner's New Orleans City Directory.*

The Bath Railroad extended to the lake, where could be found a bathhouse and Chinese pagoda/pavilion with a restaurant at what is now the location of the Bonnabel boat launch. *Author's collection.*

de Courval sold lots and squares, but by about 1837, de Courval had sold a remainder of his landholdings to Bonnabel.

By an 1838 act of the Louisiana State Congress, the Bath Rail Road Company was incorporated with Bonnabel, de Courval, James H. Caldwell (who was also involved with the New Orleans and Nashville Railroad) and others as officers. The bill stipulated that the company must build a hotel within twelve months on or near the lake equal, at least, to the one in Milneburg, and it must construct in the lake a ladies' and a men's bathhouse of corresponding value of said hotel. However, the railroad was already in existence, complete with a car house, equipment and two squares of land near the lake on which the hotel was built by Bonnabel.

In 1838, the New Orleans and Nashville Railroad also passed through Bath, where, on the lake, was a dock for transport to the northshore.

The Bath Railroad (consisting of one car pulled by horse or mule) brought passengers to the Bath Hotel. The Bath Road/tracks ran along what is now Bonnabel Boulevard. Bath Street, south of the Norfolk Southern railroad tracks, was actually a continuation of the Bath Road. The junction of the New Orleans and Nashville Railroad with the Bath Railroad was at what is now approximately the intersection of Veterans at Bonnabel Boulevards.

As for the "town" itself, the *Weekly Picayune* on October 24, 1842, sniped, "the citizen are all alligators." But that same year, an advertisement tells us that the railroad made stops at "Bath Tower," where good fishing, food and drinks could be had. The failure of Bath may be partially attributed to the same fate as the Bayou La Branche and Prairie Cottage—the loss of the railroads that had transported people there.

Lake City

After Henri Bonnabel's death, his son Alfred built a summer home on Bayou Tchoupitoulas, improved property at Bath's beach and made a lively spot for picnickers and bathers near the ancient remains of Native Americans who had created shell middens there. Alfred named the area "Lake City" and hoped that residences would also be constructed there.

Bonnabel arranged for a ferry to transport visitors and goods and from Lewisburg in the 1880s. He dug a nine-hundred-foot-deep artesian well that produced twelve gallons of water per minute at seventy-nine degrees.

"Lake City" appears on the far right of this July 26, 1914 graphic. Times-Picayune.

However, the water was not potable, which may have contributed to the failure of the enterprise as a city and a resort. A 1901 storm destroyed "Fred Bonnabel's place." John and Theodore Bruning and Marshall Hamilton rescued the family by rowing from Bucktown through the marsh in two skiffs to find that all the cattle and sheep that had grazed in the area were washed away.

BONNABEL BEACH

The completion of the first link of a planned highway from New Orleans to Hammond made the lake end of the Lake City property accessible, and what was loosely renamed "Bonnabel Beach" experienced a new era of popularity. In 1932, Alfred E. Bonnabel was making plans for a wide street (likely on the footprint of the old railroad tracks) to connect it to Metairie Road. The "Indian Mounds"/middens, the natural sand and shell beach and ancient oak trees made it a lovely spot for a picnic—the *Picayune* reported that on weekends as many as one hundred cars might be parked along what old maps labeled "Indian Beach." The mounds were a short walk from the beach or could be reached by boat on the Bonnabel Canal. They were bounded roughly by what is now West Esplanade to Twenty-Second Street and from Clifford Drive to the Bonnabel Canal.

The *Southland* Steamer

In 1923, Lake Transit Company acquired the propeller steamer *Susquehanna*, refurbished it and ran daily excursions to Mandeville and Madisonville from West End. Speedy at fourteen miles per hour, it could hold one thousand passengers. The company also bought the twenty-car ferry and freight steamship *Paul*, which it renamed *Ozone*, for the same route, and also converted the steam yacht *Reverie* (already in use on the lake) to a charter boat for parties and nightly excursions.

The company purchased the *Southland* steamboat in May 1925. The mammoth 160-by-62-foot, one-thousand-horsepower former Staten Island, New York ferry had two pilothouses (allowing it to move in either direction). The *Susquehanna* would be used for charter cruises and weekend dance cruises.

On Saturday, August 22, 1925, while about midway through its voyage from West End to Mandeville, the largest steamer on the lake, the *Southland*,

Circa 1900 photograph of the Staten Island ferry *Castleton*. The *Southland* was almost identical in appearance. *Library of Congress.*

caught fire. It was thought that a casually tossed cigarette had ignited some gasoline dripped from one of the automobiles. (The boat could hold sixty of them and one thousand passengers.) Some car engines exploded, and fire spread quickly. Folks at the Southern Yacht Club took notice and sent out alarms. Fishermen and boaters from West End to Bucktown rushed to the burning boat.

The yacht *Winnetka II*, a fifty-foot cabin cruiser recognized by the yacht club as the fastest boat on the lake (West End to Mandeville in two hours, three minutes), was captained by owner Ralston S. Cole. It happened to be cruising in the vicinity of the *Southland* when Cole noticed its distress. He and his crew rescued some sixty men, women and children from the *Southland*'s deck and lifeboats and rescued those who had jumped into the rough seas to escape the flames.

The steamer *St. Tammany* spotted the fire from about four miles away and sped to it. Its captain, James Howze, and crew helped transfer many passengers from the very crowded *Winnetka II*, and both made their way back to West End. When the passengers arrived onshore, lighthouse keeper Margaret Norvell took them into her attached residence to assess their condition. Only seven people were injured, and all of the children were unharmed.

The *Southland*, too, made its way back to the southshore but remained afire until it sunk off the shore of Bucktown. Its hull was visible for years at what is now the Bonnabel Boat Launch. It became a local landmark; the Wreck Club was named for it.

Front-page coverage on August 23, 1925, of the *Southland* fire. Times-Picayune.

East End/Bucktown

Jefferson and Lake Pontchartrain Railway

In 1840, the Jefferson and Lake Pontchartrain Railway Company was chartered to run from the city of Carrollton (then the seat of government for Jefferson Parish) to the lake along what is now the Seventeenth Street Canal. Service began in Carrollton in 1851. It later was acquired by the New Orleans and Carrollton Railway Company (aka Carrollton and Jefferson Railroad and Carrollton and Lake Railroad). A protection levee and wharf were built out into the lake, some 2,000 feet west of the New Basin Canal. On April 13, 1853, the first ride was conducted: a ten-mile trip from Tivoli Circle (later Lee Circle) along a line paralleling the Missisippi River, and then north to the lake at Bucktown and onto a 2,170-foot steamboat wharf. The trip took thirty-five minutes at a cost of twenty-five cents. At its peak, the train made as many as twelve runs per day to the "Jefferson Lake End," including fishermen's excursions.

According to a July 16, 1911 *Daily Picayune* article, "Transportation in New Orleans Fifty Years Ago," by Chris Lindauer:

> *In those days* [circa 1841] *there was a number of fine hotels at the lake end where Bucktown now stands. That is, the main hotel stood where the bridge crossed the canal, just at the inner edge of Bucktown.…* [Frank] *Roder's Hotel became as popular with patrons of the Jefferson Lake end as was Boudro's and Moreau's at Milneburg.* [Theodore] *Brunning's* [sic] *Hotel was a rival of Roder's, and the house in which this hotel was operated still stands on the mainland at the beginning of the wharf which leads to the present Brunning's Pavilion at West End.*

Jefferson Railroad Hotel

Within months of the railroad's arrival in 1853, a *Daily Picayune* notice informs us: "Jefferson Railroad Hotel—new hotel at lake end has opened rooms for lodgers.…Persons from the Lake shore, the watering places, Mobile, etc., wishing to go up or down the Mississippi without passing through New Orleans, can stop at their hotel, take the railroad to Carrollton, and there get on a steamboat." This venue, built 1,200 feet from the shoreline, was said to be large and well appointed. It was operated by Otto Briede and T.C. Roder, who called it the "Lake House" and the "Lake Hotel." In 1855, Briede bought out Roder's share of the business. In 1857, a new Jefferson Lake Hotel "fitted up in splendid style" with "airy balconies" was opened by James Benton, who remained there some eight years after the railroad ceased to bring visitors there. (In 1872, he left to open a business in town.)

Crescent Restaurant

Opened in 1853, the fine Crescent Restaurant—"third house from the hotel"—awaited hungry (or thirsty) patrons at the railroad terminus. It was operated by persons named Amodeo and Meilleur. In 1856, it was refurbished and reopened by Bonnet and Guilbeau.

Steamers

The steamers *California*, *St. Charles* and *Creole* were cruising over to Biloxi, Ocean Springs, Bay St. Louis and Pass Christian. Soon to follow were the *Rosa*, *Sazerac*, *Leonora*, *Afton* and *Florida*, all of which traveled to the northshore's "Ozone Belt." Beginning in 1856, the railroad began offering early morning fishemen's excursions.

The steamers *E. Fusilier* and *Wm. Bagaley* traveled to Mobile, Montgomery, Selma, Wetumpka and landings on the Alabama River in 1857. And in 1858, the *Virginia* and the *Creole A.* plied to Mississippi Sound ports.

In 1858, the steamer *Virginia*, getting up steam for an excursion to Point Clear, Alabama, exploded at the wharf and immediately sank. Fortunately, most passengers had yet to board, but several serious injuries and deaths resulted. The remains of the boat were raised, and in 1860, its hull was up for sale.

The railroad failed in 1864, so fewer steamboats came to Bucktown. From 1871 to 1873, the Seventeenth Street Canal was dug (actually deepened and widened, as it had existed as a borrow pit from construction of the railroad bed). In the process, the Upper Protection Levee was built along the Jefferson Parish side of the canal—both structures served to somewhat cut off the western side of Bucktown / East End from the West End. Bucktown never regained its former glory as a resort, but it became a wonderfully warm community filled with colorful, self-reliant people.

Parish Boundaries

What became known as West End was originally located almost entirely in Jefferson Parish. Before 1870, the boundary line between Jefferson and Orleans Parishes was set on the western shore of the New Basin Canal. It was then moved farther west to a strip of land slightly east of the Seventeenth Street Canal (according to the 1870 New Orleans city charter, which notes that it has annexed this section of Jefferson Parish). Neither of these boundaries were discernible to visitors to the resort; in fact, some businesses actually straddled the new line (Swanson's Seafoods, for instance).

Of note, twenty-six years later, is an August 2, 1896 letter to the editor of the *Daily Picayune* expressing surprise and dismay that the 1896 New Orleans city charter also noted this final boundary. "'Bucktown' is located some distance to the eastward of the Upperline Canal, and 'Bucktown', as we all know, is part and parcel of Jefferson," expressed the writer. This leaves the impression that Bucktown was commonly and incorrectly thought to be the location of much of the West End resort. Conversely, in later years, when the majority of the most popular restaurants were actually located in Jefferson Parish, most locals said they were "going out to eat at West End."

Perhaps to alleviate the confusion, but most likely as an attempt to make visits to Buckown more enticing (it had acquired a disreputable reputation), around 1920, some Jefferson Parish denizens, led by Theodore Bruning, petitioned Senator Jules Fischer to change the official name of the neighborhood to East End.

The Bruning Family

The Brunings were among the earliest settlers in Bucktown, and they remained prominent and influential until Hurricane Katrina obliterated everything along the Seventeenth Street Canal, including their century-and-a-half-old restaurant and beloved historic home located at the mouth of the canal's west bank, known as the "Big House."

Theodore Bruning moved his Carrollton restaurant to Bucktown in 1859 and began amassing property in the area. It is said that during the Civil War a Federal army post was established on Bruning land, where troops were quartered in hotels and sheds along the wharf, many of which were owned by him. In 1886, Bruning's Restaurant moved to the location where it remained until Hurricane Georges badly damaged it in 1998. For a time, Bruning's had dancing waitresses and rows of slot machines. In the 1880s, the restaurant was a popular Bucktown meeting place for card playing, drinking, dining and gambling. An annual event there was the Holy Thursday meeting of the BAT Club, comprising local butchers and dairymen (the acronym deriving from Butchers and Titty-Pullers). The club existed well into recent times, attracting local politicians, businessesmen and more.

In the early 1900s, J.C. Bruning owned and operated the White Squadron—forty-two white fishing boats (sixteen and eighteen feet long) that he rented for fifty cents a day. He also rented out a large dancing pavilion. In 1917, a new Bruning's Pavilion appeared in Bucktown. During World War I, the family had granted permission for a large portion of their property to be used for the temporary West End Naval Training Station. In 1924, Theodore Bruning (spellings vary: Brunning, Breuning, Bruening) claimed that his family had been granted this land on the west of the West End boat pen (now Municipal Yacht Harbor) by the Spanish government. In 1926, his widow, Amelia, won a battle against the City of New Orleans, which wanted to build a road on this property from West End Park to the New Basin Shell Road, on which she claimed ownership.

The Brunings reopened their restaurant after the destructive hurricane of 1998 in a building next door, where they served seafood, until Hurricane Katrina destroyed the West End / East End area.

The Werner Family

According to Dan Ellis (at http://neworleans.danellis.net/buck_town_usa. htm), stepson of Gus Werner, before the turn of the twentieth century, members of the Werner, Boutall and Bruning clans opened Bruning's restaurant. By 1919, what became known as "Original Bruning's Restaurant" was owned by August Frederick ("Gus/Gussie") Werner (who married Captain John Bruning's daughter Amelia), his brother-in-law Charles Arthur Boutall (who married Amelia's sister Lillian) and his father-in-law, John Bruning. Also according to Ellis, Werner owned a third of the restaurant, the Pontchartrain Plaza Dance and Gambling Hall, the Wonderland stand of gaming machines and the Bruning family home.

In 1925, Dan Ellis's grandfather Miguel Rodriguez began a hot tamale vending business (two-wheeled carts insulated with newspaper and lit by Coleman lanterns) on Bruning property. His daughter Odile "Lili" (Dan Ellis's mother) became Gus Werner's second wife in 1938. (Amelia passed away in 1934.) She continued Werner's businesses long afterward and later turned them over to Werner heirs, who owned, leased out and/or operated them into the late part of the century. These included Augie's Delago, the Bounty, the Wharf, Pontchartrain Plaza, Pontchartrain Ballroom, Lake Plaza and Club My-O-My.

Star and Garter

Some time before 1900, Joe Hyland, a well-known proprietor of gambling houses, opened the Star and Garter some three hundred feet from the parish line. It was a saloon with a gambling hall in back. Being located in the "Free State of Jefferson," it made no pretense of being anything else. A large, electrically lit star high on a pole out front served as a beacon to this notorious place.

Other Bucktown establishments popular at this time were the Phoenix Clubhouse, Flaherty's, Duke's Club, Rounder's Club, Franklin Pleasure Club, English's, Seventh District Rod and Gun Club and Monpat's bathhouse. Gambling was always popular in Bucktown, and during the 1920s, jazz made its appearance. The Venice Inn catered to lovers of both.

Swanson's Sea Foods

Frank Turan Swanson opened the Yellow Dog Saloon in 1922, serving all-one-can-eat boiled seafood for as long as one imbibed in his ten-cent schooners of draft beer. The place was a success, so, in 1926, he and his wife, Julia, opened Swanson's restaurant, which straddled the parish line—87 percent of the building was in Orleans Parish, with the remainder reserved for gambling. It was destroyed in a 1948 fire. The Swansons rebuilt with much success. Frank died in 1956, but the family continued the business until, in 1968, Vincent Aiavolasiti took over. In 1975, Bill Summers ran Swanson's Flagship here. Danny Mayer, Frank and Julia's grandson, decided to take the reins in 1978, but he passed away the following year, and the doors to Swanson's closed for good. The building burned to the ground in 1984.

Fitzgerald's

In 1915, Margaret Bruning and Maurice J. Fitzgerald celebrated their wedding at the Bucktown home of her parents. In 1932, they opened Fitzgerald's Seafoods Restaurant on the little site that would later become Maggie and Smitty's Crabnett, later moving to a larger, seven-thousand-square-foot building at 1928 West End Park. Their son and daughter and their spouses joined the ranks. For a time, there were gambling and slot machines as readily available as the fried softshell crabs and boiled seafood. In 1960, the wide porches were enclosed and a thirty-ton air conditioner was added—gone were the lake breezes. Hurricane Hilda damaged the restaurant in 1964, but the family repaired it and kept it going strong. Margaret and Maurice celebrated their fiftieth wedding anniversary there in 1965 at the ages of sixty-seven and seventy-eight, respectively. Margaret passed away in 1966. Maurice died in 1976. Shortly after, it was run by Henry F. Bonura. Maurice Jr. later took over the kitchen and management and ran it very well, but by 1989, the glory days of West End had come to an end. He sold the restaurant in 1989; it continued in operation until Hurricane Georges (1998) damaged it beyond repair.

Wonder Bar / Club My-O-My

Emile Morlet opened the Wonder Bar at 125 Decatur Street in 1933, featuring male entertainers impersonating female performers. In 1936, after the city declared it a menace to morals, Morlet relocated to East End on the west side of the canal in Herman Brunies' former Family Restaurant. It was renamed the Wonder Club, which later became the Club My-O-My. A 1948 fire destroyed the My-O-My and Swanson's while damaging Bruning's, Grover's and Iacoponelli's. The My-O-My was rebuilt as a small, one-story, iron-roofed, 34-by-76-foot building. In 1956, the club moved to the Werners' old Pontchartrain Plaza venue (see following page). After another move or two, the last of East End's Club My-O-My burned in a 1972 fire that also damaged Kirsch's seafood restaurant next door.

Ralph Uribe photograph of the 1972 fire that destroyed the last East End Club My-O-My. Times-Picayune.

Pontchartrain Plaza / My-O-My / The Bounty

Gus Werner died just months after opening the over-the-lake Pontchartrain Plaza gambling house and dance hall in 1948. Lili continued the business, which later became Pontchartrain Ballroom, then Lake Plaza (in 1954). With seating for two thousand, it was allegedly one of the largest dance floors in the South. Sunday "Mambo Matinee" dances were popular here in 1955.

In 1956, Club My-O-My moved into this much larger venue after the Orleans Levee Board took over its former location. After damage from Hurricane Hilda (1964), My-O-My moved to the south portion of the former Kirsch's Seafood Restaurant. The original Pontchartrain Plaza remained vacant until 1968, when Lili had it up for rent: a ballroom able to accommodate 1,000, a dining room, a lounge and a kitchen. The building burned down to its pilings in 1969 and was rebuilt by the Werners as the Bounty, a large building able to accommodate 1,200 patrons. In 1991, it became the Mutiny.

The White House Restaurant

Charlie Watson's White House bar and restaurant at 422 Hammond Highway opened in 1947, and it became a popular venue for seafood, beer and gambling. In the early 1970s, Benny Compagnano ran it as Benny's White House and brought in live orchestras for dancing. James O'Connor acquired the place in 1974 and operated it again as the White House.

In 1981, after thirty-four years, a fire damaged the building. O'Connor developed plans to build a fifteen-story, forty-eight-unit condominium on the site, which would include the property of Charles Turan's adjoining abandoned shrimp processing plant. Ten years later, Turan acquired the White House property, and the condo plan was floated again. A decade later, after years of wrangling over zoning variances and historic integrity, a condo went up in 2002. The $15.5 million, thirty-unit, seven-story Fleur du Lac complex offered panoramic views of the lake (while blocking them from longtime residents) at an average cost of $500,000 per unit. Pontchartrain Place condos were built adjacent to it. The Brown Foundation built a third high-rise between Seminole and Mayan.

Maggie and Smitty's Crabnett

Brother and sister Marguerite and Lloyd ("Red") F. Hemard opened the Crabnett in 1962. Elaine ("Smitty") was their sister and nonworking partner. Maggie (who had worked at Fitzgerald's) and Red (an electrician by trade) produced gumbo, boiled and fried seafood and poor boys in a tiny indoor kitchen with a small dining area and offered a larger outdoor seating area as well.

Maggie and Red persevered through years of storm damage, the general demise of the 1980s and even Hurricane Georges in 1998, which took out Bruning's and Fitzgerald's. But after the death of Red in 2001, the old landmark closed down. Many remember the cats who were welcome to dine there. Some old-timers still swear by Miss Maggie's gumbo and Mr. Red's seafood platter.

"Restoration" and a Parking Problem

Cars were literally "stuck in the mud" in 1973 after heavy rains turned the western end of West End Park into a swampy mire. And so a $250,000 plan to convert the muddy shell-covered space in the center of the restaurant area into a pedestrian "mall" was conceived. Benches, landscaping, lighting and paved parking for 240 cars were components of a larger project to renovate the entire park. In years past, east of the restaurants, a fountain, a swimming pool, outdoor seafood and watermelon stands and other attractions had been popular.

Due to the Jefferson Parish / Orleans Parish boundary conundrum, this was to be a joint effort of the New Orleans Parkway Commission and the parish of Jefferson. Some argued that even more parking was needed, but planners deemed that additional parking would only result in longer waiting times at the restaurants.

Other components of this 1973 plan included a linear bike park, a four-hundred-foot-long pier and the closure of the "Gap Bridge" at Orpheum Avenue over the Seventeenth Street Canal to vehicular traffic. In 1976, the old wooden bridge that had accommodated as many as one thousand cars per day was closed to autos. It had been the primary route to and from West End Park for Jeffersonians.

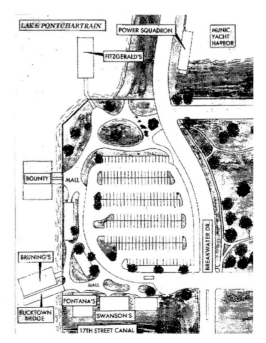

A graphic published on December 9, 1973, of a plan to improve the Jefferson Parish portion of West End Park. Note the restaurants existing at that time. Times-Picayune.

The pedestrian mall was still a work in progress when Jefferson Parish president Douglas A. Allen likened the proposed results to the ambiance of Monterey, California's Cannery Row and San Francisco's Fisherman's Wharf. Work finally began in 1976 on the now $433,135 project, 60 percent of which would be paid by Orleans Parish, which, in turn, would receive the parking fees. The plan now called for three hundred parking spots; management of the lot was put up for public bidding.

By June 1977, four years after the plan's inception, the parking lot was under operation, but to the dismay of restaurateurs, their businesses were in trouble. Sam Urrate of Bruning's reported that his revenue was down by a third, as was that of Henry F. Bonura's Fitzgeralds. Co-owner John L. Fury of the Bounty Restaurant and Nightclub said his income was down $3,000 in a recent weekend alone. Dominick "Papa" Roselli was losing 50 percent of his business—and so was the restaurant's bread delivery driver. The company leasing and managing the parking lot was in dire straits, too; not only was the parking lot relatively empty, but also many of the cars in it had avoided paying the $1.06 two-hour fee by exiting through the entrance or driving over curbs designed to envelop the lot. The bottom line was that regular patrons did not care to pay to park in a locale that had never charged before. And many families simply couldn't afford the additional charge.

The restaurants never fully recovered from this blow, even after parking fees were later waived. The only saving grace of this debacle was that the beautiful old oak trees lining the area were left standing. The old Gap Bridge has now been replaced by the massive post-Katrina drainage pumps.

Augie's Delago

In the late 1970s, Augie Werner (Gus's son) and his brothers Ed and George Werner built a platform over the lake next to Fitzgerald's. Plans called for it to be named after Gus's old Pontchartrain Plaza, but instead they named it Augie's Delago, which opened in 1979. It gradually grew to three stories with ten bars open 24/7, four docks and two bands playing on separate floors. After Augie's had its heyday, the Werners leased it to a concern in 1987, which called it the Yacht Club. During the early morning hours of Memorial Day 1987, the building burned down. Business there had been poor, and the building was falling into disrepair; the Werners had been granted permission to demolish it.

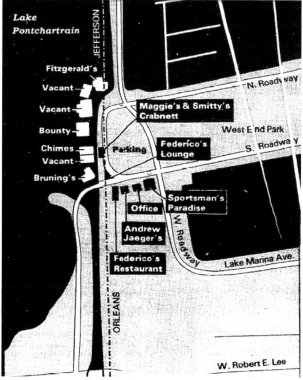

Above: Augie's Delago, circa mid-1980s. *John DeMajo.*

Left: Businesses existing in East and West End (note the parish line) in 1987. Times-Picayune.

But in 1988, the Werner brothers were busy building a new "Delago on the Lake," a platform used in 1990 as Joe Sobol's Sunset Sam's, an open-air venue with a bar, two bandstands, barbecue pits and free parking. The place stayed open until 3:00 a.m. In 1992, the property—which by then consisted of a 12,875-square-foot wharf with a 1,000-square-foot building on it—was for lease. The next year, a new Augie's was begun here, just as the first had, but larger. Now it was a 35,000-square-foot open deck with a covered bar. It hosted bands and a Halloween "Haunted Wharf" featuring Elvira the Mermaid, Swamp Man and Octopus Man. The location was later sold to become Jaeger's Beer Garden.

Sid-Mar's

Sid-Mar's began on Harrison Avenue in 1967 before Sidney and Marion Gemelli Burgess moved to 1824 Orpheum in 1972. Before their arrival, the old place had been Lenfant's bar, Ferdie's, Emken, Dee's, Bee's, Buddy Fuchs and Maybeth's. Marion cooked great Italian (including a wonderful Wop salad) to go along with the fried and boiled seafood. Cold beer, screened porches and Lake Pontchartrain sunsets were all a part of this unpretentious, utilitarian ambiance.

In the mid-1970s, Marion was one of the founders of the annual modern-day Fourth of July Bucktown Blessing of the Fleet, with its old-time pirogue races. Sid-Mar's served as its unofficial headquarters, with proceeds donated to Children's Hospital. World War II veteran and Purple Heart recipient Sidney Burgess passed away at the age of seventy-seven in 1993. Marion and their son Kent continued to run the restaurant until Katrina washed it away. Marion died in 2013 at the age of eighty-eight.

8

WEST END

We of to-day cannot fail to realize that West End originated, planned and perfected in a spirit of enterprise and liberality by the City Railroad Company.... Nowhere else in the United States, probably nowhere in the world, has any private or public corporation extended favors and opportunities to be compared with those now offered by the liberal and public-spirited present administration of the City Railroad Company.
—Daily Picayune, *March 26, 1882*

There can be little doubt that the preceding was written by someone under the employ of the New Orleans City Railroad Company. Despite its gross exaggerations, the fact remains that, like most of the other early resorts, this one relied, for a time, on a railroad for its existence. But at its inception and for the first thirty-eight years, there was no railroad to West End. From 1853 to 1864, the Jefferson and Lake Pontchartrain Railway to Bucktown / East End was certainly used by folks whose destination was West End, but it was not until 1876 that the subject of this chapter's epigraph (New Orleans City Railroad) began service to West End.

Located two miles west of Spanish Fort, it was originally called the New Lake End, located at the end of the New Orleans Navigation Canal / New Basin Canal, a shipping channel that opened in 1838 (the year the New Canal Light station was established). A shell road ran three straight miles along the western shore of the canal, so flat and smooth that horse and carriage racing along it was a popular pastime. Some of the first to

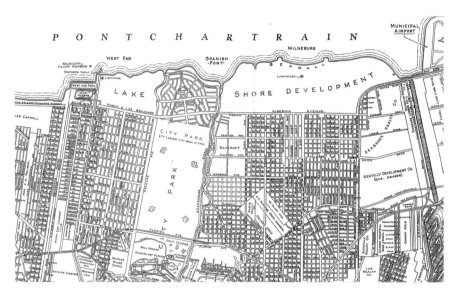

This 1931 map illustrates major features of West End (*top left*) that remain today. However, much has been lost. *Author's collection.*

use it were the earliest denizens of West End: the Wave Club and the Lady of Lyons rowing clubs, which built their boathouses on the canal in the mid-1830s. By 1844, there were two passenger barges plying the canal, pulled by horses on the shell road, for a fare of twenty cents each way. A city ordinance outlawed horse racing on said road. By the 1850s, the canal was loaded with vessels carrying sand, lumber, gravel, shells, watermelons and other goods.

CANAL EXCHANGE

Henry Roder opened the New Canal Coffeehouse and Restaurant some time before 1838 "on the Lake End opposite the hotel." By 1852, he had the Canal Exchange and provided not only food and lodging but also a ten-pin alley, a pistol gallery, a bar, a bathhouse and buggy rides provided by horses in his stable.

The Lake House

In 1838, the Lake House restaurant and hotel, owned by the New Orleans Canal and Banking Company (which had built the canal), was under construction. It opened in 1939, and its manager, Henry Bax, enticed visitors by serving ice cream every day at 4:00 p.m. In 1840, an omnibus was chartered to deliver folks from town to the establishment on Sundays. Also that year, Lewis A. Reed ran the hotel. Dan Hickock took over in 1848, when the Lake House was said to rival the finer places in Milneburg. In 1853, George W. Cullum was the new lessee, touting delectable pompano and mullet. Dan Hickock returned in 1855, but by 1861, Dan Peters and Company was running the show. In 1863, W.B. Smith managed the Lake House at what was known as (Dan) "Hickock's Landing." The following year, Charles J. Hoyt took the job, running the hotel, its shooting gallery and garden while also adding new bathhouses and a long wharf out into the lake.

An 1870 fire, allegedly set by disgruntled employees, destroyed the thirty-two-year-old, three-story, wood-framed structure along with Hoyt's furnishings. In 1872, an elegant new Lake House was opened by Hoyt and Theodore Bruning. In 1874, Hoyt petitioned to be allowed to build a hotel in front of the protection levee that ran along the western side of the Seventeenth Street Canal. By 1877, he was operating the Lake Hotel, until around 1893.

Lucien Boudro's Hotel

Lucien Boudro operated a hotel and restaurant that was built on the shell road in the 1840s, before and after he made his name at Milneburg. Cod fish and lobsters fresh from Boston were on his menu in 1845. After an 1849 fire, he moved back to Milneburg.

Franklin House

In 1845, Franklin House was built along the canal by the banking company and operated by persons named Hunter and Lathrop, who served pompano, terrapin, oysters, softshell crabs and more. Dan Hickock ran it for a time and hosted a regatta here in 1849.

1860s–1870s

In 1867, the city took over the resort after the railroad and harbor venture failed in Bucktown. An eight-hundred-foot embankment was built, extending out the mouth of the canal. The city also filled a 1,200-yard area from Jefferson Parish to the canal, one hundred feet wide and eight feet high. A huge wood platform was constructed over the water, and a hotel, restaurant, gardens and other amusements were added.

An 1870 advertisement suggested, "to promote your health…take a daily drive to the New Lake End over the shell road." In 1873, the Canal Street, City Park, and Lake Railroad was granted permission to extend its track (which ran from the city to Spanish Fort) to New Lake End and Milneburg, along the lakeshore, with the right to use the lakeshore embankment "if desirable for two years thereafter" in a twenty-five-year charter. In 1874, Toney's House saloon and restaurant between the shell road and Upper Protection Levee had wide, breezy galleries on which to serve pompano, Spanish mackerel, croakers, wine, liquors and cigars.

An 1874 article described the carriage route to West End and what to do while there:

> *out Canal street to the Half-Way House* [located at City Park Avenue, which at that time was named Metairie Road, and Canal Street], *and thence by the shell road to the New Lake End. The road is in good condition shaded by tall overhanging trees. On top of levee is a pedestrian promenade, room for a double track city railroad, and a broad carriage road. It will extend along the whole lake front. Go to refreshments and these at the LAKE HOUSE, Charley Hoyt, dinner or supper, with croakers, sheephead, red fish, pompano, crabs, oysters and the finest meats, choicest finest wines and attentive, courteous waiters. After this you can take another stroll on the levee, a bath if you wish and drive home by moonlight every evening in the week.*

In 1875, the excursion steamer *John Wise* was cruising the canal, as was Captain Cochran's steamer *Margaret*. In 1876, the New Orleans City Railroad Company extended its route from Canal Street at Metairie Road to West End and erected a jail near its offices. Brown's House (which had shooting matches) was located on the canal. On the east bank near the lighthouse, the St. John Rowing Club built a two-story headquarters with porches on three sides in 1877, when Charles Lacoume was constructing a saloon. The 1870s ended with twice-weekly Grand Promenade concerts by the Crescent City Battalion Brass Band under the direction of Oscar Wolff and sponsored by the railroad, which had built a pavilion for just such an event.

TRANCHINA'S AT WEST END

Tranchina's restaurant opened at West End around 1878. The *New Orleans Item* wrote of Tranchina's in 1893, "Their elegant dining parlors are fitted up in due Parisian style and their cuisine contains everything succulent to tempt the delicate palates of our most iconoclastic gourmet." Around 1897, it became Tranchina & Olivieri's restaurant. In the early 1900s and the 1910s, Terrence Tranchina was also the hotel keeper at West End. In 1913, Tranchina was located both here and at Spanish Fort, but this would be his last year at West End.

In this undated rendering, we see (*left to right*) Tranchina and Olivieri's restaurant, an unidentified building out in the lake, the bandstand, the scenic highway (roller coaster) and Mannessier's confectionery. *Louisiana Digital Library.*

ASTREDO'S

In 1878, John Astredo's Hotel and Restaurant was built on the levee and out into the lake, three stories high. This would later become the Crescent Hotel.

1880s

Around 1880, the New Lake End was becoming known as "West End," and the train consisted of a motorcar pulling open carriages past the St. John's Rowing Club to a landing platform and a new drawbridge to the West End Garden and Promenade. There, one could rest on a bench, enjoy flower beds with shade trees and at night be guided by electric lights to the likes of Dick Brown, "The Champion Banjo Soloist of the World." A new West End Hotel was near completion, and a large, open pavilion on the wharf east of the hotel was planned, as were six pagodas to be built along the lake side of the revetment levee (which was a half mile long from the New Canal to the upper protection levee in Bucktown).

The lakeside revetment was deemed a "nice esplanade," which ran parallel to a second shell road and promenade bordered with rows of oaks, willows, crape myrtles and flowers. A lagoon in back (later to become the Municipal Yacht Harbor) was destined to have islands and bridges spanning it.

All seemed well, but Professor Sporer's band, it was said, was "selecting music totally unsuited for a resort of this kind." The powers that be retorted: "The selections…are the finest classical pieces of the best masters, similar to the selections…played in the Central park, New York. The musical critic of the Times would probably prefer lighter pieces.…Are we never to make any progress in musical taste in New Orleans? Are we forever to be gagged with the doggerel style of music?"

The West End Rowing Club, in 1880, met at the Crescent Hotel to plan the building of its boathouse, and in 1881, it was done—two stories, complete with a reading room, a bathroom, a ladies' parlor, a main room downstairs for boats and equipment and a second floor of dressing rooms for the 160 members. The St. John regatta of 1880 drew a heavy crowd of about 5,000 people, many of whom filled the drawbridge. Heavy winds halted the races, but not the party with its brass band and food and drink. An 1880 fireworks display included a three-foot hexagonal wheel of "Japanese fire" and a finale of NOCRR (New Orleans City Rail Road) aglow amid parachutes, stars, rockets and bombshells.

The Pontchartrain Regatta Association had its first contest in 1881, when Professor B. Moses (who for the previous two years had been at Spanish Fort) and his orchestra were the West End "house band" for the season and the trains were running nonstop to a new depot near the St. John boathouse.

The French Consul was there in 1881 for a Bastille Day celebration with speeches (in French and English), a concert, a regatta, dancing, fireworks and a one-hundred-gun salute. When all was done, some of the crowd of fifteen thousand waited some seven hours to return home, as the trains were packed each time they were loaded. The festival was such a success that the organizers returned to West End for several years after.

In 1882, Samuel Clemens visited New Orleans and spent time out and about with George Washington Cable at West End, when more than three thousand multicolored Chinese and Japanese lanterns were strewn all through the resort—at the depot, on buildings, over the bridge, on bushes, on statuary, on benches and for a mile down the revetment in an attempt to create a Coney Island–style atmosphere. And in that same year, a benefit to raise funds for an Army of Tennessee tomb took the form of a reenactment

POLO RACE AT THE WEST END

An 1881 Bastille Day celebration included an exhibition water polo match whereby players rode on wooden barrels topped with horse heads. *Author's collection.*

of the Civil War Battle of Shiloh—the New Basin Canal bridge was taken by the "Federalists," and the "Confederates" retreated down the revetment levee as a veteran Rebel soldier shouted "Tigers!" Former Confederate president Jefferson Davis was in attendance.

In 1883, the resort was described as being quite lovely, with elegant structures, beautiful walks and gardens and, of course, wonderful views of the lake. In the center of it all was a fine pavilion that served as the bandstand, where the railroad contracted Professor G. D'Aquin to provide classical music for the season.

E.F. Denechaud's luxurious West End Hotel (which was protected by its own twenty-member fire company) housed a theater and hosted a free concert and ball in 1883. McCloskey's Pavilion went up that year, serving carbonated drinks, mead and cakes. A professional bicycle tournament pitted three racers vying for a prize.

In 1886, one of the country's first Switchback Railways (gravity-powered roller coasters) was built on the bank of the canal, heading out into the lake. The 1887 summer season promised a complete renovation and the employment of Professor G. Sontag's orchestra for evening concerts. In 1888, the popular fifty-eight-member Mexican Band (from the recent World's Cotton Exposition in Audubon Park) played along with the forty musicians of the West End Band—a total of ninety-eight musicians blasting tunes along the shoreline in free concerts. Now West End had a reliable railroad, hotels, restaurants, promenades, beautiful gardens and good swimming and bathing facilities. Along the lakeside shell road to Bucktown were restaurants, shooting galleries and more, but the hedge-laden Puzzle Garden maze was a major attraction (especially for lovers), with its grottoes and statuary. It was in this decade that West End was first touted as the "Coney Island of the South."

First Motion Picture in New Orleans

In 1886, Allen Bruce Blakemore, electrical engineer for the railroad, tamed the five-hundred-volt streetcar mainline that extended from the tracks and over the basin, to light the large bandstand out in the lake. A string of bulbs was lighted by running the current through a barrel of water and to an Edison Company Vitascope machine. A seven-by-ten-foot screen was placed on the bandstand, and on June 28, 1896, at 8:00 p.m., New Orleanians

A scene from the *The Kiss*, an early motion picture viewed by New Orleanians in 1886. *Thomas A. Edison Inc.*

viewed their first "moving pictures." On the hand-cranked machine was played a series of "shorts"—sequences that lasted up to sixty seconds or so. (The first full-length movie wasn't made until 1903.) Of all the "pictures" shown that evening, the most popular by far was the Edison Company's twenty-second sequence, *The Mary Irwin Kiss*. Costar John C. Rice took his time wooing Mary until the climax, when he twirled his mustache just before planting a three-second kiss, accompanied by West End's house musicians in Paoletti's Concert Band.

1890s

In the early 1890s, storms damaged the revetment and tore up the boardwalk. Proprietors were overwhelmed and allowed the park to fall into further disrepair. Several fires during this decade added to the woes. In the late 1890s, entertainment included the Bellstedt-Ballenberg Concert Band (Professor Herman Bellstedt had just composed the "Southern Yacht Club

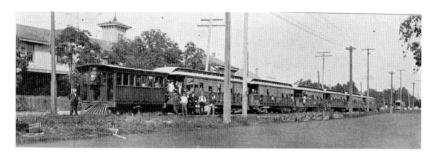

The West End Railway in 1891. *Carnegie Library of Pittsburgh.*

Mannessier's, opened by Paris native Auguste Mannessier on Canal Street in 1852, moved to Royal Street near the courthouse until, after seventy-two years, it closed in 1914. Under his name, the business was operated at Spanish Fort and at West End from about 1899 until 1912. *Library of Congress.*

Here we see the Southern Yacht Club, the roller coaster and the lighthouse beyond it in 1901. *Detroit Phtographic Company.*

March"), the vitascope, the specialty performances of magician Albini, Miss Nellie Maguire's character songs, Bessie Bonehill ("a handsome woman and a charming artist, who will do her famous impersonations and character change acts"), as well as birds brought over from the Ostrich Farm on City Park Avenue. The entertainment was becoming as dismal as the place.

1900s

In the early 1900s, West End streetcar conductors walked along a railing on the outside of cars to collect fares. Canvas curtains were rolled down to protect passengers from inclement weather along the route from Canal Street to the cemeteries, then along three miles of the canal. This was the fastest route in the city at twenty miles per hour, powered by four sixty-five-horsepower motors. (The St. Charles line had only two of these.) Small sheds perched over the canal about a quarter of a mile apart (every two or three blocks) were the stops—at Mound, Homedale, Florida, Brooks, Polk, Ringold, Harrison, Lane, Fillmore, Mouton and Spanish Fort Road (now Robert E. Lee Boulevard). In 1950, the streetcar was replaced by a bus.

In 1900, the Mystic Swing attraction fronted Tranchina's. The thrill involved being placed in a moving seat surrounded by rotating scenery, which gave the illusion of being flipped and turned. *Detroit Photographic Company.*

The Ferris wheel, scenic highway, mirror maze and other carnival-style amusements were popular. A 1901 storm ripped out half of the land that had held the puzzle garden. In 1903, Armond C. Veazey's Military and Concert Band entertained, along with vaudeville acts. Attractions in 1905 included Schepp's mini-horses as well as "Queen and Bunch," the educated canines. Fishers Band played here regularly in 1906. By 1908, the resort was in bad shape, dilapidated, decaying and overgrown with vegetation. The two public bathhouses were in disrepair, but Tranchina's and Mannessier's pavilions were well maintained. A devastating storm in 1909 badly damaged Mannessier's roof, broke windows and skylights and tore some fifty feet off the train shed and tossed it into the steamer *Ozone* and the tugboat *Expert*.

The Capitol Hotel opened around 1900. *New Orleans Public Library.*

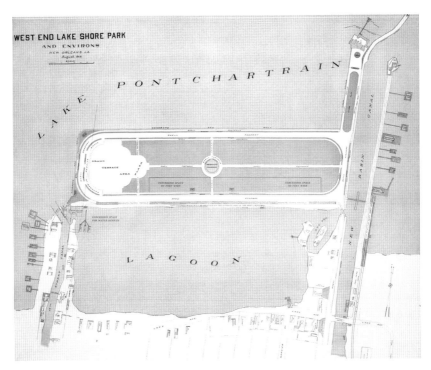

West End Park in 1914 included the prismatic fountain, the Grand Terrace, shell footwalks and roadways, an auto parking area and concession spaces. *Library of Congress.*

1910s

West End was closed in 1910. The next year, the city took over the railroad's expired lease with plans for improvements. Tosso's Military Band did perform there that year, but the bandstand, casino and other buildings were removed. And that was the end of West End as a true resort area. However, the streetcars remained in operation, and the old wooden platform built over the lake was used for rides, concerts and vaudeville acts.

In 1915, the city built new picnic shelters but began leasing the former resort for more private business endeavors. An electric prismatic fountain was introduced in 1917. In 1918, Ralph Levey's Japanese Garden (a self-described "local roadhouse…a very sumptuous affair") popped up near West End Park.

West End Tavern

Around 1918, the West End Tavern was located near the recently established U.S. Navy Training Station. In 1943, it was the Swing Club, featuring Santo Pecora and his Swing Orchestra (including Clyde Hurley, formerly with Glenn Miller) for two floor shows nightly. In 1955, Sophie Johnson took over and renamed it the Lake Air Tavern, hosting seafood parties and banquets. In the 1980s, at 8500 Pontchartrain Boulevard, it was the Windjammer restaurant.

West End Roof Garden

West End Roof Garden, opened in 1919 at 7600 West End Boulevard under the auspices of the posh Hotel Grunewald (later the Roosevelt), was a lively Roaring Twenties fancy dance and dining venue. In 1920, Lerdo's Mexican Orchestra was not only the house band but also played free public concerts. The College Six Jazz Band was there in 1921, as was Tony Parenti's Orchestra in 1922, when a children's garden was added for picnics. Carhop service offered some of what was provided inside from the café, soda fountain and snack bar. In 1923, Burt Earle's Famous California Orchestra was accompanying the newly released silent movie *Java Head*. A 1924 raid resulted in the New Orleans assistant district attorney being arrested for possession of a quart of whiskey, but no other hootch was found on the premises.

Pinky Vidacovich was a favorite here in 1925. In 1926, when the Grunewald became the Roosevelt (which retained ownership of the Roof Garden), the New Orleans Owls became the house band, playing its popular "West End Romp" and entertaining the audience with hijinks of all sorts.

The venue was closed for a couple of years, but in 1930, it reopened to host the Blue Parody Orchestra and, in 1931, music by the Oreos. In 1932, the Roof Garden became the Bungalow, providing dining and dancing to Earl Bard and his Orchestra. Sidney's Southern Syncopators were there in 1933. In 1935, it became the West End Roof Bar. Still in operation until about 1956, this once-famous venue faded away, but not before having hosted such jazz greats as Papa Celestin and Kid Ory.

1920s

By the early 1920s, the amusement rides and many concessions were gone. The prismatic fountain was working again when a new playground and four water fountains were added. Free public weekly concerts were given by Rosato's and Harry Mendelson's military bands; reportedly, more than three thousand people attended on any given Saturday. Camps still lined the lakefront. A 1921 picnic at the Lillian cottage for employees of Fuerst and Kraemer candy company was in the news—it was its third annual outing and included music by the Tuxedo Jazz Band. For the general public, free Sunday concerts were given by Emile E. Tosso's orchestra.

Jazz venues included the American Club, Bienville Roof, Bruning's Tavern, Dixie Cottage, Lakeview Park and Lillian Cottage. A few of the bands that performed at West End were Fishers Band, Papa Celestin's Tuxedo Band and the Maple Leaf Jazz Band. Musicians included Norman Brownlee, Ti Boy Gilmore, Monk Hazel, George Henderson, Tony Jackson, Yank Johnson, Steve Lewis, Joe Loyacano, Andrew Morgan, Sam Morgan, Joe "King" Oliver, Happy Schilling, Kid Thomas, Clarence "Little Dad" Vincent and Joe Watson. In 1928, Louis Armstrong paid homage with his recording of "West End Blues."

1930s

When Milneburg, then West End, lighthouse keeper Margaret Norvell passed away at age seventy-one in 1934, the *Times-Picayune* reported on the front page, "Woman Who Rescued Many from Storms Crossed the Bar, Starts on Sea of Eternity." She was beloved by many. That same year, six thousand bushes of roses of sixteen varieties were planted on trellises. In addition, a new shrub/puzzle maze and magnolia trees were planted. The roses were removed in 1964.

The 1936 WPA guide tells us of "West End Park, 'Bucktown,' and the Southern Yacht Club...several night clubs...concrete sea wall... shade trees...refreshment stands where crabs and shrimps are served in season." It continues with a lovely description of the fountain: "A special attraction is a large fountain in operation during the summer months. Here people sit for hours on warm nights watching the play of the waters in various colors, each spray an individual representation.

A look at the workings of the prismatic fountain, 1941. *Louisiana Digital Library.*

One of the loveliest of these is known as the 'Prairie Fire,' a fountain of water illuminated by gold, red, yellow, and blue lights."

By 1937, the six-and-a-half-mile Lakeshore Drive was completed along the shoreline all the way to Shushan Airport (as it is today). The year 1938 brought plans and WPA funding for the Municipal Yacht Harbor (which was done) and a new lighthouse (which wasn't). In the late 1930s, Kelly's Seafood at 7612 West End Boulevard had waiters and carhops. During the 1940s, it became the Lake Breeze Inn and then Blue Streak Enterprises, a boat retailer.

GROVER'S RESTAURANT

Grover Schiffer's place was raided in 1947 to reveal twenty-one slot machines, which were summarily destroyed. Before this was accomplished, New Orleans authorities studied maps to ascertain which establishments were in Jefferson Parish (not their jurisdiction). Swanson's Seafoods restaurant was seven-eighths in Orleans; its gaming machines in Jefferson Parish were spared that fate.

1950s–2005

As part of the new Union Passenger Terminal's transportation plan, streetcar tracks along the New Basin Canal were removed and replaced with buses. The last streetcar ride to West End was in 1950. The canal itself was being covered over, but in 1952, it remained open between Florida and Robert E. Lee Boulevards. In 1956, a three-day Lake Pontchartrain Fishing Rodeo attracted 1,500 people to West End to vie for $6,000 worth of prizes.

In the late 1950s, the New Basin Canal was filled to become the Pontchartrain Expressway/I-10, as well as Pontchartrain and West End Boulevards and the massive neutral ground between them. During the 1950s and until Hurricane Katrina's destruction in 2005, West End was largely neglected, aside from the parking lot/restoration in the 1970s.

However, along the remains of the canal sprang up the Hong Kong, Ichabod's, Barts, the Dock, Joe's Crabshack and Landry's restaurants, which thrived. West/East End restaurants, in later years, included Chimes, Federico's, Spinnakers, the Happy Buddha, NeoBeach and Sportsman's Paradise (to name just a few). Coconut Beach (formerly NORD's Mickey Retif playground) was a popular venue for sand volleyball. They, too, are all gone.

And so ends our virtual trip to places lost around Lake Pontchartrain. One can only imagine what the future holds.

Post Hurricane Katrina, in the public areas of East and West End, all that remains are the oak trees that were spared more than a generation ago when the parking debacle ran its course, the broken balustrades topping the old protective bulkhead and the pilings upon which restaurants stood and memories were made. *Google Maps.*

BIBLIOGRAPHY

BasinStreet.com. http://basinstreet.com.

Chronicling America: Historic American Newspapers. Library of Congress. http://chroniclingamerica.loc.gov.

Ellis, Frederick S. *St. Tammany Parish, L'autre Cote du Lac.* Gretna, LA: Pelican Publishing Company, 1981.

Hyland, William de Marigny. "A Reminiscence of Bernard de Marigny, Founder of Mandeville." Speech given before a meeting of Mandeville Horizons, May 26, 1984.

New Orleans. http://neworleans.danellis.net.

Tammany Family. http://tammanyfamily.blogspot.com.

Times-Picayune (New Orleans, Louisiana). NewsBank. https://infoweb.newsbank.com/apps/news.

INDEX

ABOUT THE AUTHOR

An LSU graduate with a BA in fine arts, Cathy chose a career in teaching (MEd, University of New Orleans). She became a school technology coordinator and early proponent of the educational value of the Internet. New Orleans History—Lake Pontchartrain (www.pontchartrain.net) was her first attempt to compile a cultural overview as a pictorial history of the lake. *Lake Pontchartrain* (Arcadia Publishing, 2007) culminated this endeavor in a print edition. Now a retired educator, Cathy's interest in writing and research has grown to include the books *Metairie* (2008), *New Orleans City Park* (2011), *Legendary Locals of Metairie* (2013) and Images of Modern America: *Lake Pontchartrain* (2015), all released by Arcadia Publishing, as well as her more recent *Lost Metairie* (2017), published by The History Press.

Cathy and her husband, Mike Azzarello, are the parents of two children and the grandparents of two adorable children. Cathy hopes this book will inform, educate and rekindle wonderful memories of life around Lake Pontchartrain.

Visit us at
www.historypress.com
....